Austin Clarke was born in Dublin's Manor Street in May, 1896. He was educated at Belvedere College and University College, Dublin. His first publication was a long poem *The Vengeance of Fionn* which appeared in 1917 to critical acclaim and went into a second edition. From then until his death in 1974 Clarke published some twenty volumes of poems, over half of them published under the Bridge Press imprint in limited editions of about two hundred copies, three novels *The Bright Temptation* (1932), *The Singing Men at Cashel* (1936) and *The Sun Dances at Easter* (1952), all of which were banned by the Irish Censorship Board, two volumes of reminiscences *Twice Round the Black Church* (1962) and *A Penny in the Clouds* (1968) and over a dozen verse plays.

In 1932 Clarke was elected a founder member of the Irish Academy of Letters, became its president in 1952 and received its major literary award, the Gregory Medal, in 1968. He spent some seventeen years in England where he reviewed books in various papers such as the *Daily News and Leader*, *The News Chronicle* and *The Spectator*. Returning to Dublin in 1937 he reviewed books for *The Irish Times* (1940-1962 and 1968-1973) and *The Irish Press* (1962-1968) and had a weekly poetry programme on the national radio station Radio Eireann for about thirty years.

A PENNY IN THE CLOUDS

A Penny in The Clouds

MORE MEMORIES OF IRELAND AND ENGLAND

Austin Clarke

MOYTURA PRESS
DUBLIN

First published 1968 by
Routledge & Kegan Paul Ltd,
London.

This edition published by
Moytura Press, 3 The Dale,
Stillorgan, Co. Dublin.

© R. Dardis Clarke 1990

ISBN 1-871305-03-9

This edition was printed by
Colour Books Ltd., Dublin

Contents

Acknowledgements

Acknowledgements and thanks are due to the following for permission to quote from published work:

To Mrs. Yeats and Messrs. Macmillan for quotations from W.B. Yeats's work.

To Estelle Starkey for poem and prose of Seumas O'Sullivan (James Starkey); to the relatives of the late Philip Francis Little; to the Rev. Lawrence Wilson for Robin Wilson; to Oliver Gogarty, B.L., and to Terence de Vere White and the Shaw Bequest for an uncharacteristic postcard of G.B. Shaw.

I have not been able to trace the literary executors of Victor Plarr.

One

EVERY MORNING at the top of the Leader Column in *The Freeman's Journal* was to be seen as headpiece a small drawing of the Irish Houses of Parliament against the rays of the rising sun at College Green. This eighteenth-century building with its graceful colonnade really faced the east, but it seemed proper that the sun should rise symbolically in the west, so eloquent were the members of the Irish Party at Westminster. All through my early years, the word 'Nationalism' shone in my mind, despite those who mocked at patriotic speeches and denounced them as 'sunburstry'.

During the Summer of 1912, after I had left school, I studied both for the National University entrance examination and a Municipal Scholarship. For the latter, young applicants had to submit an essay on the Parliament of Grattan and Flood. I read many library books and explored the era of the 'Protestant Nation', of which I had never heard at our Jesuit College. I triumphed with Grattan, I despised Flood, who had accepted the post of Vice-Treasurer in 1775. My mind rang with great phrases of Anglo-Irish oratory, such as the exclamation of De Burgh when the Irish Volunteers were formed: 'England has sown her laws like dragon's teeth, and they have sprung up armed men'. I peered through smoke at the Volunteer regiments ranked in College Green, presenting arms as the Earl of Charlemont reviewed them, while a salute of cannon reverberated from street to side-street. Much later, I found that Charlemont had been a fastidious scholar and published a volume of fine translations of sonnets by Petrarch.

On the first day that I arrived at University College, Dublin, a constituent of the National University of Ireland, I was filled with awe. A tall, keen-faced man, with a small, pointed white beard, was talking to someone at the kerb. I recognized him at once from a newspaper photograph. He was Professor Swifte McNeill, member of Parliament, who had written a concise study of our eighteenth-century Parliament. I was surprised when I entered the hallway of the large Georgian house, for inside, it might have been one of the Commercial Colleges around it in St. Stephen's Green. Neither professors nor students wore cap and gown. Our special classrooms were in a row in an annexe, little better than a shed, opposite a small railed-in garden. The schoolrooms I had known were more spacious. Worse still, our philology and Old English classes were held around a deal table, in an attic of the main building and we climbed to knowledge by dirty back-stairs. Only gradually, did I realize that after Catholic Emancipation had been gained, the Church hastened to install itself in great buildings. But I was unaware of the rise of a wealthy Catholic middle class, and as I sat, notebook in hand, in attic or garden-shed, I thought that our country was still poor and distressful.

So, I was astonished, during my second term, by the Lock Out of 1913, when English Labour unions sent a ship from Liverpool to bring over children from the Dublin slums in order that they might be fed and cared for during the long struggle of the workers against the Catholic employers. False cry of proselytism rang from every pulpit, echoed from the servile newspapers, re-echoed around breakfast tables. In our Literary and Historical Society, earnest second- and third-year students rose to their feet to denounce the wickedness of Socialism.

On my way home, I usually avoided the Houses of Parliament – now the Bank of Ireland – for, if I glanced across the street, I might see, with envy, undergraduates flaunting in cap and gown at the gateway of Trinity College. Nevertheless, I was tempted at times to come that way from my classes, so that I might stare into the bookshop windows in Nassau Street and Dawson Street. I had become vaguely aware of Irish poetry, because the volumes of W. B. Yeats were displayed in them, some open: their covers still lavish with the gold-leaf which had been used in the nineties to adorn the Book Beautiful. Moreover, in the art shops down Grafton Street, his best-known lyrics, such as 'The Lake Isle of Innisfree' and 'When you are old and gray', hand printed, illustrated, were on sale. Later, I saw the framed poems on the drawing room walls of every house with pretensions to good taste.

I borrowed the early *Collected Poems* of Yeats from a Municipal

2

Lending Library, and groped through the Celtic Twilight, confused by the delicate impressionism and images. Vainly, I tried to scan the poems, but they evaded the prosodic rules which I was learning in our classes. Only after I had read a great deal of English literature did I appreciate the subtle, delayed rhythms.

So, when I left College in the afternoon, I made my way by back streets, crossing from Cuffe Street to Ship Street, Nicholas Street, past Christ Church, down Winetavern Street, over the Liffey Bridge to the Four Courts, along Smithfield, into Red Cow Lane, Grangegorman, and so to my home on the North Circular Road.

II

The streets were bright with spring sunshine as I stole into the Abbey Theatre for the first time. I had hesitated so long at the corner, watching the last of the small crowd hurry to the Saturday matinee, that I was already several minutes late. In some vague way, I had heard of Irish drama and its traditions, for knowledge of outside affairs comes painfully and confusedly to a young student living in the shadow of examinations. Scarcely had the programme seller taken my ticket at the door of the pit when she disappeared into what seemed complete darkness. I groped my way after her, full of alarm and bewilderment, for from the Stygian gloom came the most lamentable outcry that I had ever heard in my life.

As I grasped the back of a seat and sank down, I could make out dimly on the stage two robed figures. When my eyes became accustomed to the gloom, I saw that they were standing before an immense locked gate. At first, in my confusion, I thought that this must be some ancient tragedy and that these two shadowy figures were stricken souls in Hades. But gradually, I realized that they were shawled women and that this unabashed hullabaloo was the famous 'caoine'. It seemed to me as if the dismal Muse of Irish history were present, adding her own groans to those embarrassing cries. The shock of that sudden encounter with Irish tradition was so great that to this day, I cannot remember what play followed *The Gaol Gate* by Lady Gregory. But the experience was so strange and exotic that I determined to return again.

In those years before and during the Great War, the literary tradition of the Abbey was not as yet in complete abeyance. The hilarity of farce was controlled, if not in kind, at any rate in time. The farces were shorter and were always preceded by a serious one-act play or a poetic play by Yeats; sometimes the order was reversed and farce was confined to the curtain-raiser. Inordinate laughter is so complete an experience in itself that we rarely remember what brought those stitches to our sides, those contradictory tears to our eyes. Memory requires some violent jolt from the past to stir it into activity. So I remember best of all that moment in *A Minute's Wait* when an infuriated goat held up the one-way traffic on the West Clare Railway. Did a well-trained billy-goat really rush across the stage, scattering market women, farmers and decrepit railway officials? Or was it only a scuffle in the wings which left that indelible moment of idiotic mirth in the mind?

But the plays of Yeats were a deeply imaginative experience, and, as the poet put on his own plays as often as possible, the experience was a constant one. On such occasions the theatre was almost empty. There were a few people in the stalls, including Lady Gregory, and just after the last gong had sounded, Yeats would dramatically appear at the top of the steps leading down into the auditorium. Perhaps the actors spoke the lyric lines in tones that had become hollow-sounding with time, borrowing the archaic voice which is normally reserved for religious services. It seemed right that the poetic mysteries should be celebrated reverently and with decorum. Moreover, the presence of the poet himself in the theatre was a clear proof that all was well.

Scarcely had the desultory clapping ceased, when Yeats would appear outside the stage curtain, a dim figure against the footlights. He swayed and waved rhythmically, telling humbly of his 'little play', how he had rewritten it, and what he had meant to convey in its lines. As the twenty or thirty people in the pit were more or less scattered, I was isolated usually in one of the back seats. On such occasions, I felt like Ludwig of Bavaria, that eccentric monarch, who sat alone in his own theatre. I enjoyed the poet's curtain-lecture, almost as if it were a special benefit performance for myself.

One night, however, my youthful and romantic illusions were suddenly shattered, and in a trice the Celtic Twilight was gone. As

4

the poet appeared punctually outside the curtain, a dazzling light shone around him. It might have been the light of his later fame! I glanced up and saw that the brilliant shaft of illumination came from the balcony. A spotlight must have been clamped to the rail and switched on as the poet appeared. But my conclusions may have been unjust, for in youth we do not understand the complexities of human motives. I did not realize at the time that poetic drama was slowly vanishing from the Abbey Theatre. It seems to me now that, consciously or not, the poet might have been making a last despairing gesture to call attention, not to his own picturesque person, but to the struggling cause of poetry on the stage.

I saw a performance of *The Countess Cathleen* once only. The very first lines have a simplicity and imaginative quality that is new:

Mary: What can have made the grey hen flutter so?
Teigue: They say that now the land is famine-struck
           The graves are walking.
Mary: What can the hen have heard?
Teigue: And that is not the worst; at Tubber-vanach
           A woman met a man with ears spread out,
           And they moved up and down like a bat's wings.
Mary: What can have kept your father all this while?
Teigue: Two nights ago, at Carrick-orus churchyard,
           A herdsman met a man who had no mouth,
           Nor eyes, nor ears; his face a wall of flesh:
           He saw him plainly by the light of the moon.
Mary: Look out, and tell me if your father's coming.

The words spoken by Aleel and the Countess Cathleen are both lyrical and dramatic.

Cathleen: He bids me go
           Where none of mortal creatures but the swan
           Dabbles, and there you would pluck the harp, when
               the trees
           Had made a heavy shadow about our door,
           And talk among the rustling of the reeds,
           When night hunted the foolish sun away
           With stillness and pale tapers. No – no – no!

5

I cannot. Although I weep, I do not weep
Because that life would be most happy, and here
I find no way, no end. Nor do I weep
Because I had longed to look upon your face,
But that a night of prayer has made me weary.

I liked best the sparse language of *The King's Threshold*, a play
which, despite the critics, I have always thought dramatically
effective on the stage.

Seanchan: Yes, yes, go to the hurley, go to the hurley,
Go to the hurley! Gather up your skirts –
Run quickly! You can remember many love songs:
I know it by the light that's in your eyes –
But you'll forget them. You're fair to look upon.
Your feet delight in dancing, and your mouths
In the slow smiling that awakens love.

The mothers that have borne you mated rightly
They'd little ears as thirsty as your ears
For many love songs. Go to the young men.
Are not the ruddy flesh and the thin flanks
And the broad shoulders worthy of desire?
Go from me! Here is nothing for your eyes.
But it is I that am singing you away –
Singing you to the young men.

No doubt, the poet should have written 'hurling' instead of 'hurley',
which is the stick or 'camaun'. I had not realized at the time that
'ruddy' and 'lineaments', which are used later in the play, were
favourite words of Blake. And here are some well-known lines from
On Baile's Strand:

Ah! Conchubar, had you seen her
With that high laughing, turbulent head of hers
Thrown backward, and the bowstring at her ear,
Or sitting at the fire with those grave eyes
Full of good counsel as it were with wine,
Or when love ran through all the lineaments
Of her wild body – though she had no child,

6

None other had all beauty, queen or lover,
Or was so fitted to give birth to kings.

The most exciting play which I saw in those early days at the
Abbey Theatre was, ironically enough, not an Irish one, but a
Continental experiment in dramatic impressionism. It was *Hannele*
by Gerhardt Hauptmann, a play in two scenes. When it first
appeared in the 'nineties' this small play caused a sensation. It
infuriated critics in Paris as a sample of German infantilism, and
was denounced as blasphemous in New York. It depicts, with all
the relentless compassion of Hauptmann, the delirium of a child
rescued from drowning and brought to a workhouse hospital.
Reality and hallucination mingled in the strange scenes; sacred and
profane figures dissolved into one another. It was all a confused blur
to me at the time, but I realized instinctively that the play was a
protest against the oppression of the young and that insidious sense
of spiritual guilt which is instilled by custom into the adolescent
mind. It was a first glimpse of analytical drama. Another memorable
experience was the production of *The Post Office*, by Rabindrinath
Tagore. His play expressed religious intimations, not with that
familiar emotionalism which dulls understanding, but in new
images, cool, clear and surprising.

I was fortunate in catching the last of that imaginative movement
which inspired so many writers here and in seeing all of Yeats's
plays before they disappeared from the theatre he had founded. So
I remember gratefully that sunlit Saturday when I stole into the
Abbey Theatre for the first time and heard with astonishment the
wailing women.

III

A narrow up-and-down road between hills a few miles beyond
Wicklow town led to Brittas Bay, a lonely place of dunes with its
twelve miles of beach. Horse-and-cart went along the winding road
and sometimes a Ford motor car passed, leaving behind it a cloud
of dust that hid the hedges. In July 1914, when I went there on
holiday with my sisters, the summer was remarkably fine and we
had a month of continuous sunlight. Every morning I left the

7

old-fashioned guest-house, the only one in that isolated district, and hurried across the bracken to lie among the dunes. There, each day I read a canto of Spenser's *Faerie Queen*. It was a dreary task, and as I moved slowly from stanza to stanza, knights and ladies went dimly along my mind. Little did I suspect that there was a political allegory in the poem, though I was aware only too well of the moral one. After that, I added a few stanzas in common measure to a long poem which I was writing about the mystery of the astronomical world around us. Then, released from task and poetic duty, I hurried with my togs across the warm slopes of sand to the beach and swam in the sea.

One morning, I opened the book at the fourth canto and read the opening stanza with its elaborate simile –

> Like as a ship with dreadfull storme long tost,
> Having spent all her mastes and her ground-hold,
> Now far from harbour likely to be lost,
> At last some fisher barke doth neare behold.

The sun shone so eagerly, the waves were making such a pleasant noise along the hidden shore, that I could not resist undressing. I climbed the nearest sand-hill, slipping and plumping, until I came to the top. I stood in astonishment, for, a mile away, was a sailing ship. It looked sinister, waiting there in the bay. I forgot Spenser and remembered the pirate stories I had read as a schoolboy. After my swim, I stayed on the beach watching the mysterious three-master.

After lunch I came back to the dunes. The ship was still motionless in the middle of the bay, though its sails were spread. I suspected that the captain and crew were waiting until dark to unload a cargo of contraband. I roamed the miles of beach and sand, still glancing back at the strange vessel.

I did not tell my sisters about what I had seen, but late that night, I was back again among the dunes. The ship was still there, the moonlight gleaming on spar and yard. I watched it until almost eleven o'clock when the careful old lady locked, bolted and chained the halldoor of the guest house. Through the silence, came the rasp of the fern-owls as I stole back. I lingered under the porch for a few minutes in the sultry twilight, enjoying the fragrance of the trestled jasmine.

8

Long after midnight, I was wakened up by the roaring of Ford cars and of gear changing, unusual sounds in those years. I did not realize that it was an historic event – the first gun-running in the South. Sometime previously, arms had been landed on the northern coast by the Ulster Volunteers under the leadership of Sir Edward Carson.

A few weeks later, on an unforgettable evening, all the round of the sky was aglow with the light of a startling sunset, as I crossed the small bridge over the stream on my way to the dunes. The air through which I moved, slowly and as gently as I could, was glorified. I seemed to be lost in an ethereal world for all the latitudes were fiery. Sunrise in the west and sunset in the east were mingling, and the vaulted sky above was all radiance. For the first time, I understood A. E.'s poetry of the heavens:

> Its edges formed with amethyst and rose,
> Withers once more the old blue flower at day;
> There where the ether like a diamond glows,
>   Its petals fade away.
>
> A shadowy tumult stirs the dusky air:
> Sparkle the delicate dews, the distant shows;
> The great deep thrills, for through it everywhere
>   The breath of Beauty glows.

and again:

> When the breath of twilight blows to flame in misty skies,
> All the vaporous sapphire, violet glow and silver gleam
> With their magic flood through the gateway of the eyes:
>   I am one with the twilight dream.

This poetry of celestial hues, of jewels dissolving into light, recalls the Apocalyptic school described by Rémy de Gourmont in *Le Latin Mystique*. Later, I came on 'Lotus and Jewel' by Sir Edwin Arnold, with the mystic word *Om* in gold on a green cover. The book was published in 1891 and I have often wondered whether A. E. knew the poems in it about jewels such as Fire-opals, Amethyst, Nacre and Pearls, Diamonds, Jacynths, and Topazes:

Across the Aramoean sands across
The Erythoean billows; syenite,
Black porphry purple-veined, the satin gloss
Of onyx; coral, crystals, chrysolite.

With abaci of silver. I will have
A milk-white warm pavilion in the midst,
Such as Siddartha, Prince at India, gave
To bright Yasodara.

I wandered along the shore beside the gleaming waves. Soon I wanted to talk about the wonder to someone and came back between the dunes to the roadside.

Old men were outside the cottages, their faces unearthly. All of them were shaking their heads: 'It's a bad sign, something terrible is going to happen.' I left them and went back to the sandy hollows. Far away, I could hear the rasp of the fern-owls as the heavens slowly dimmed. The next day at noon when the newspapers came, we learned that Germany had invaded Belgium. The Great War had begun.

IV

The centenary of Thomas Davis in 1914 was to be held at Trinity College, Dublin, but the meeting was banned by the Provost, Dr. Mahaffy, and in scornful words, which caused much indignation to Republicans, he referred to 'a man called Pearse' who was to be one of the speakers. So the meeting was held in the Ancient Concert Rooms in Brunswick Street, later to be renamed Pearse Street after the Insurrection.

The long dusty hall downstairs was almost filled when I arrived but I found a seat halfway down. Already on the platform were W. B. Yeats, who was to deliver the oration, Padraic Pearse and the young chairman, Denis Gwynn. One chair was still empty. I scarcely recognized the poet of the Abbey Theatre whom I had seen so often coming before the dim footlights on the stage after one of his plays had been performed. Gone were the flowing tie and the disobedient black lock that fell over his brow as he talked and swung

10

back into place whenever he lifted his head. He was in evening dress and his long hair had been oiled and brushed back. This gave a saturnine look to his olive features so that he seemed to be extraordinarily like Sir Edward Carson, who was then the fearsome Dublin-born leader of the Unionist party in the North. Scarcely had Yeats started to speak when, on the right hand side of the hall, there was a sound of heavy footsteps on the bare boards. It was the missing poet, Captain Thomas Kettle, braving us in the uniform of a British officer. He marched up the hall so firmly that we almost seemed to hear the clatter of his sword but it was obvious that he had his fill of Irish whisky in order that he might defy more confidently this small group of Sinn Féiners.

When Yeats rose to speak, I wondered how he would deal with the poetic problem of the Young Ireland School of the 'forties, the rhetoric of those political and historical ballads of Davis, D'Arcy Magee, Gavan Duffy and other poets whom he had attacked – the jingle of their double rhymes, of which perhaps the worst was the constant rhyming of 'Ireland' with 'Sireland'. But the poet had been wise enough to choose the one poem by Davis which could lend itself to his own thrilling sort of chanting: 'The Lament for Owen Roe.' As he rose to his full height, swayed and, with waving hands, intoned the poem, his voice spread in rhythmic waves throughout the hushed hall.

Did they dare, did they dare, to slay Eoghan Ruadh O'Neill?
Yes, they slew with poison, him they feared to meet with steel,
May God wither up their hearts! May their blood cease to flow!
May they walk in living death, who poisoned Eoghan Ruadh!

The audience was overcome with enthusiasm and when he sat down again there was great applause. But before that there had been as much clapping when, by a simple device which I noticed at the time, he brought in irrelevantly the name of Nietzsche, for the German poet with his philosophy of the Superman was regarded with horror in all our pro-British press during the First Great War. I felt annoyed for I had been reading with guilty delight *Thus spake Zarathustra*, *The Joyful Science* and *The Birth of Tragedy* with its fascinating theory of Dionysiac and Apollonian moods.

Padraic Pearse followed. I had only heard vaguely of him and of

St. Enda's, the school which he had at Rathfarnham, one of the few lay schools left in Ireland. This forlorn experiment had been resented by the Archbishop, who refused to appoint a chaplain for the pupils. There, with his sculptor brother, William, Thomas MacDonagh, Padraic Colum and other poets, he taught, and there was no corporal punishment as in the religious schools throughout the country. Even today, although it is illegal, cane or leather are used in National schools, colleges and convents.

Tall, pale, aloof, dressed in a black suit, Pearse spoke with an intense lofty devotion which stirred me uneasily for it was a cold impassioned rhetoric which was new to me, and carefully declaimed. Later he expanded the thesis of his brief speech in his essay on Davis which is one of the four pamphlets called *Tracts for the Times*. In this he wrote – I am almost certain that he spoke the words at that meeting in the Ancient Concert Rooms in 1914:

> The real Davis must have been a greater man even than the Davis of the essays, or the Davis of the songs. In literary expression Davis was immature; in mind he was ripe beyond all his contemporaries. I cannot call him a very great prose writer; I am not sure that I can call him a poet at all. But I can call him a very great man, one of our greatest men. None of his contemporaries had any doubt about his greatness. He was the greatest influence among them, and the noblest influence; and he has been the greatest and noblest influence in Irish history since Tone. He was not Young Ireland's most powerful prose writer: Mitchel was that. He was not Young Ireland's truest poet: Mangan was that, or if not Mangan, Ferguson. He was not Young Ireland's ablest man of affairs: Duffy was that. He was not Young Ireland's most brilliant orator: Meagher was that. Nevertheless 'Davis was our true leader', said Duffy; and when Davis died – the phrase is again Duffy's – 'it seemed as if the sun had gone out of the heavens.' 'The loss of this rare and noble Irishman', said Mitchel, 'has never been repaired, neither to his country nor to his friends'.

And Pearse added: 'The Romans had a noble word which summed up all moral beauty and all private and civic valour: the word *virtus*. If English had as noble a word as that it would be the word

12

to apply to the thing which made Thomas Davis so great a man'.

When Captain Kettle rose to speak, a tumult broke out at the back of the hall and a tall red-bearded man, who looked like Darrell Figgis, jumped to his feet, angrily shouting. Captain Kettle, who was to die so soon at the Battle of the Somme, kept shouting in reply to the heckler, 'Where was your father when mine was in prison?' The miseries of the Land War, the ramming of clay cottages, the evictions, boycotting and shooting of landlords from behind hedges with buckshot, the assassinations in the Phoenix Park of the Secretary of Ireland and his companion, were around us. The vision was all the more vivid because my father had once brought me to see Skin-the-Goat, who had driven the assassins to the Park. He had been given a job as night-watchman by a grateful alderman of the city.

When the meeting was over, I waited outside and saw Yeats go by with half a dozen friends. He stood talking with them for a few moments and then all walked slowly towards Westland Row. My sudden suspicion that Yeats had cleverly captured that small audience of rebels proved correct.

Next morning the placards appeared with the startling caption: DUBLIN AUDIENCE CHEERS NIETZSCHE.

Two

I

ONE EVENING, early in 1915, if I remember rightly, I went to a public lecture given by St. John Irvine in the Vegetarian Restaurant, a pleasant place near College Green in Dublin, long since vanished. Mr. Irvine was Manager of the Abbey Theatre at the time and, in speaking of drama, dealt with the touchiness of our audiences and compared us unfavourably with our countrymen in the North. I was a Second Year Arts student at University College and that day, the Assistant Lecturer in English, Thomas MacDonagh, who was afterwards one of the poet-leaders of the Easter Week Rising, had lent me a slim volume of verse. It was one of the Poetry Book Shop publications, either *The Old Ships* by James Elroy Flecker or, as I think, a reprint of his earlier poem *The Bridge of Fire*. At the time I knew scarcely anything about contemporary poetry and was very pleased to have a loan of this brand new chap-book with its bold lettering on the title page. I suspect that I carried it rather ostentatiously for, as the crowd was leaving after the lecture, a tall young man, round-faced, and with rimless glasses, stopped me and said in a polite, Protestant voice: 'Excuse me, is that Elroy Flecker's *Bridge of Fire* you have?' That was how I met the future Manager of the Abbey Theatre. We walked part of the way home together and I learned that he wrote poetry and was a clerk in the office of Brooks Thomas, a large building firm. His name was F. R. Higgins.

F. R. Higgins and I became close friends and went for long walks at night time along the Green Lanes of Clontarf, now a residential area, or chatted in small Italian cafes over Camp coffee and penny cakes. We were both eighteen, but I was awed by his knowledge of the 'Nineties, the Celtic Twilight, Symbolism, and Maeterlinck for at that time Yeats was still known as the Celtic Maeterlinck. He discoursed on Japanese poetry; lent me Victor Plarr's little book on Ernest Dowson. It was all confusing, exciting and stimulating to me

14

for I had only a knowledge of academic literature and had not got much farther than Tennyson. I had also some academic knowledge of Gaelic poetry and for that reason was all the more puzzled by Celtic Twilight Impressionism. I do not think Higgins ever asked me about the poems which I was trying to write: they were too bad to show to anyone and so I listened reverently as, along the dark hedgerows, he walked with me intoning some of his earliest delicate lyrics. Even then he was constantly reshaping and rewriting them.

On one memorable occasion Higgins decided to share a secret with me. He would show me a wonderful pool, which was to him a symbol of Immortal Beauty, for in those years beauty was not, as we say, a dirty word. I was thrilled for now at last the perplexities of Symbolism would be made clear to me. It was a misty night. Suddenly the young poet stopped and pointed out to me near the roadside his symbol. I saw in the fitful light of the moon, beneath a few bare trees, a muddy hollow. I said nothing but to that sudden shock I trace back my dislike for the Symbolist movement.

Higgins composed even his early poems to the rhythm of Irish airs and ballad tunes. Like Colum, Campbell and the poets of the previous generation, he was much influenced by the delicate Love Songs of Connaught, collected and translated by Douglas Hyde. He had spent his childhood in Foxford, County Mayo and spoke often of the little river-gardens along the Moy and of gathering wild strawberries at Ballivor, County Meath, where he stayed at times with his father's relatives. His early poems were based on those memories, in the city, of a country childhood. Awed, I shared his lyric mood as he spoke of sloe bushes, hazel nuts, the bright eye of the hunting otter; and I wondered what he meant when he sang of:

> The flush of Helen's wine
>   On ghostly nudities,
> On cold men herding swine
>   By wasted seas.

Higgins told me little of his home life but I knew there was strain. His father, a railway employee, was a strict Unionist, but Fred had been swept into the nationalism of the literary movement. Indeed shortly after we met, his father turned him out because he refused to join up and fight for King and Country and so he had to live in lodgings. Thus one of his finest poems 'Father and Son' written long afterwards, came from a deep conflict of emotion over the years. The quiet of its delicate speech-rhythm prepares us for its mood of reunion.

> Only last week, walking the hushed fields
> Of our most lovely Meath, now thinned by November,
> I came to where the road from Laracor leads
> To the Boyne river – that seemed more lake than river,
> Stretched in uneasy light and stript of reeds.

Anger is good. I think discipline, meditation, may be better.

Differing in our religious upbringing, Higgins and I learned from one another. One summer's evening, we went to see the great rhododendron display open to the public at the Howth Demesne. We lingered on in that Caucasian sunset of blossom. In a quiet spot, Higgins climbed up until he was hidden and read out the Song of Songs, while I lay luxuriously on the ground under the petals. I had known only the Douai version and the notes that assured readers that this voluptuous poem was really an allegory of the future Church. But as that voice rang out from the blossoms, I knew indeed that it was the poetry of polygamy and written by a poet who had a hundred wives.

> Thy lips are like a thread of scarlet,
> And thy speech is comely
> Thy temples are like a piece of a pomegranate
> Within thy locks.
> Thy neck is like the tower of David builded
> For an armoury
> Whereon there hung a thousand bucklers,
> All shields of mighty men.

Higgins was not only a poet and convert to the Sinn Féin movement, he was also a pioneer of the Labour movement. As a student I had been only dimly aware of the grim conditions when the Lock Out of 1913 happened and the employers, led by William Martin Murphy, supported by the Church, endeavoured to starve out the workers. Soon after I knew him, Higgins founded the

Clerical Workers' Union; he told me that he was instantly dismissed from his employment. He was given a small salary as secretary of the Union, but funds were low – clerks were still timid – and so, for all his dream-life of the country, the poet had to face the problem of earning his living. He showed much practicality, ingenuity and cheerfulness. He was the first to found a woman's magazine in Ireland. It lasted about a year. Then with the same genial hope, he persuaded our printing firms to produce trade journals and when one failed, he started another.

One evening, over our Camp coffee and our cake, Higgins explained to me that the disestablished Church of Ireland still kept the tradition and simple services of the early Celtic Church. As I knew little about ecclesiastical history, I was impressed by his knowledge and the powerful arguments which he had been taught. To that talk behind a wooden partition in a plain cafe, I owed my later interest in the neglected Celtic-Romanesque centuries.

Both of us longed to meet a real poet and we took a tram several times to the Rathmines Town Hall, near which was the small chemist's shop owned by James Starkey, better known to us as the poet, Seumas O'Sullivan. We bought a tin of Zambuk, another of Vaseline, a box of Beecham's Pills, in the hope that the poet would be behind the counter or dispensing at the back of the shop. But he was never there.

So, in desperation, we made our way one afternoon, when Fred was on holiday, to the public-house in Patrick Street, owned by P. J.McCall, who had written 'Follow me up to Carlow' and other rousing ballads. There were no drinkers in the bar when we came in. He ordered two small ports, and we stole admiring glances at the poet, who was about forty years of age, curly-headed, handsome as John MacCormack, the great tenor. Fred, in his manly way, talked about racing and sport to the poet, as he dried tumblers expertly and then mentioned casually a Wexford ballad. The poet modestly changed the conversation. Fred was not to be deterred, so he talked of the Love Songs of Connaught, which had been collected by Douglas Hyde. Again, the poet dodged us and talked of the Irish favourite for the Grand National. After a while, he happened to remark that the Boss was at home in Clontarf with a bad cold. We realized that we were talking to the barman.

Hastily, we left that public-house.

17

Often F. R. Higgins and I went to Artane where Mrs. Reddin held a *salon* every Sunday. I had been to school with two of her sons, Norman and Kenneth. Their mother had made a happy discovery in Armagh of an old ballad with a pretty refrain:

> The lambs on the green hills
> Stood gazing at me
> And many's the ship on the ocean
> And strawberries grow by the salt sea.

At nine o'clock, guests trooped into the dining-room where an ample cold supper was laid on the long table. At one end was an enormous baron of beef, at the other end an equally enormous one of corned beef. There, I met Edward Martyn, whom I had often seen near the Kildare Street Club, dressed in a reefer, with jaunty sea-cap, looking as if he had left his yacht around the corner. One evening a guest at supper boldy asked him whether he had ever read *Hail and Farewell* in which his great friend, George Moore, had depicted him as an absurdly comical character. 'Good heavens.' he exclaimed, 'I wouldn't dream of doing so'. Cardinal Logue had replied with similar surprise, when asked if he had read *The Countess Cathleen* before damning that play in public.

On a showery Sunday afternoon in May, I went with the Reddins on a pleasant drive through North County Dublin, where Nathaniel Hone had painted wide skies, that seemed to spread beyond his canvasses. We stopped at a roadside cottage, and I turned to a youth of eighteen called Michael Willmore, who had come with us. He was a promising artist and had already illustrated two books, one by Padraic O'Conaire, the other by Daniel Corkery. To my astonishment, he was radiant in sunlight. I remembered, then, that he lived at Howth, where Diarmuid and Grainne, in the old legend, had hidden in a sea-cave from the pursuit of the Fianna. Diarmuid of the Love Spot had been blessed in the same way when Aonghus, the God, appeared to him.

Later, that raysome youth won fame as an actor, under the Irish form of his name, Mícheál Mac Liámmóir.

Three

STRANGELY ENOUGH, I cannot remember how I first met Stephen MacKenna. He was not widely known in his own lifetime, although scholars and literary critics acclaimed his rendering of the *Enneoads* of Plotinus into English as one of the great translations of our age. When he started his task, which took him twenty years, many had avoided the re-editing and translating of the philosophic work, because they did not wish to risk their reputations, owing to the grammatical difficulties and obscurities. The adventure was undertaken by an ex-clerk and struggling Irish journalist, who had forgotten his school Greek. 'In the army of scholarship MacKenna was destined to fight to the end as an irregular', wrote E. R. Dodds, Regius Professor of Greek at Oxford, in a Memoir of his friend. Lacking a university degree, he was forced to complete his labours against hardship and poverty.

In his translation, he set himself against what he called wittily 'the Verral-Jebb-pseudo-grand-days-of yore-is-a-sham'. His Journal written in the peaceful days, of 1908 shows how worthily he prepared himself:

> For years I played foolishly with 'The Phrase', seeking the bubble 'self-esteem' even in the canon's teeth, defying all the sanctities if only I might anyhow please myself with a yell and a flare and a fit of ribald glee: now only I begin to know that it is not 'The Phrase' that counts to any good, it is 'La Phrase'. Hence, the orderly suave and gracious setting of the true mood is the clear meaning. This is the anatomy of style as anatomy is the beginning of medicine and of surgery, of painting and of sculpture. The glory is to come later, if it ever comes: as a man must first be sober before he can be a saint, and learn to behave himself before he climbs into the pulpit.

Stephen MacKenna was an almost legendary figure in the literary circles of Dublin. He had shared scanty meals with Synge in Paris, fought for the sacred soil of Greece in the Turkish War of 1897, swept out a restaurant for a livelihood in New York. As a journalist he caught the eye of Pulitzer, the newspaper magnate, and had been appointed Continental correspondent in Paris with a staff of assistants and a large salary. He cast the post aside with a magnificent gesture and returned to Dublin to pursue his studies in Greek and Irish. More than all this, in a city where conversation was still recognized as an art, this moody scholar was an incomparable talker, astonishing all with his imaginative eloquence.

He had some amusing oddities and was not always aware of the noisy outside world. Robert Donovan, my professor of English at University College, who had been a Leader writer on *The Freeman's Journal*, told me of a characteristic example of MacKenna's absent-mindedness, when he was on the staff of that paper. News had just come in that the missing Dr. Crippen had been arrested on a charge of murder on his way to the United States, and a radio message – the first of its kind – had been relayed to the Liner. MacKenna was asked to write a leaderette on the subject. He went over to the reference shelf to look up the name Crippen in an Encyclopaedia.

George Moore shocked his 'conservative' neighbours in Ely Place by having his halldoor painted a patriotic green. MacKenna offended a highly respectable suburb by his queer taste in music. I called to his house in Anglesea Road once and was told in awed tone, that Mr. MacKenna could not possibly be disturbed. It was the sacred Thursday evening when his concertina teacher gave him and James Stephens an hour's lesson in the attic.

Once, in writing a letter to him, I addressed it to Stephen McKenna, Esq. In reply I got an indignant postcard informing me that he spelled his name with a 'Mac' not with the Kaffir 'M or 'M.K'. From its rhythmic sentence-run, it was clear that the same postcard had been dashed off and dropped into a pillarbox many times.

When I met MacKenna, he seemed to be in easy circumstances, and I assumed that his American wife, Marie, had an income. Often in the afternoon, I went to see him and he would rouse himself from his melancholic mood and start talking in his impassioned way on many subjects, snatching up whatever book he was reading at the time. He defended, for example, the complimentary songs of the eighteenth-century Gaelic poet Carolan, showing me how the occasional, irregular rhythms were due to his improvisations on the harp. He declaimed passages from Rabelais so powerfully that the onomatopoeic effect of the monkish compounds and nonsense words in the mighty parody were clear to me.

He spoke Irish fluently and in a Dublin way. Once I listened for half an hour while Mrs. Alice Stopford Green, the historian, and he conversed so eagerly that it became a living language to me. Later he taught Irish to James Stephens, and to his enthusiasm and help, we owe *Reincarnations*.

Stephen MacKenna, who suffered from ill-health, was tall, black-haired, languid in his movements. Nevertheless, his deep musical voice became vibrant as it moved onward in sombre eloquence. I asked him once about his experiences in London during the Nineties, but he disliked the great city and dismissed it in one of his vivid sentences: 'In the middle of Piccadilly Circus, a navvy would get down from a cart, open his trousers, take out an organ as large as that of an elephant, and proceed to piddle against the back-wheel.'

I regarded Stephen MacKenna as my literary father, but he was a difficult parent and I did not always venture to visit him, for his moods were uncertain. He had praised excessively my first book. So when my third book was published, I went to see him at Bray where he was staying to recuperate. 'I've a golden boil on my bottom', he exclaimed, rising painfully from the cushion on an armchair. He pushed aside *The Sword of the West* with an impatient gesture, 'I couldn't get through it'. He talked of other subjects, with sore halts, his first alliterative exclamation coming as a refrain, much to my confusion for I was young and outwardly modest.

II

After the Irish Treaty was signed in 1921 and a Provisional Government set up, Stephen MacKenna, who remained a Republican, was so indignant that he left the country at once. At the same time, that caustic critic and Unionist, John Eglington, left for contrary reasons. Both settled down sharing their grievances, in Bournemouth.

At the first Tailteann Games in 1924, a prize was awarded to him, which he refused to accept in a violent letter. But the wily promoters of culture suppressed the letter and got that 'innocent essayist', G. K. Chesterton, who was over for the occasion, to present the prize *in absentia* to the unwilling translator of Plotinus.

I met Stephen MacKenna by chance one morning in the tea-room at Victoria Station. He had come up from Bournemouth to see the wealthy patron, who subsidized the translation, and was having breakfast, of tea, toast and boiled egg. He was dressed for the great occasion in a suit of dark blue, with a nice new tie. Unfortunately, in the middle of the tie was a blob of yolk. Such was my awe of him, that I did not dare to tell him. He seemed incapable of finding his way to Addison Road, and so I brought him there on the bus. Still worrying over that yellow blob and my lack of courage, I left him at the gate of the lordly mansion. That was the last time I met Stephen MacKenna.

III

On a sunny afternoon in the Spring of 1915, I ventured hesitantly along Oakley Road, in Ranelagh, and found after a brief search the address for which I was looking. The front garden of the small Georgian house was gay with daffodils between the ornamental shrubs. The door was opened by a tall young woman, pale, red-lipped, with heavy black hair and languorous movements. In a Rossettian dream, I waited for a few moments in the drawing-room, until her husband, Thomas MacDonagh, came in and greeted me.

I had met the poet once or twice in College, although I was not as yet in his class. I saw him often making his way happily among the throng of students in the hall, small as Thomas Moore, and as curly-headed, speaking vivaciously with quick gestures. He dressed in light grey, wore a brown bow, a round hat clapped back.

He was Assistant to Professor Robert Donovan, a white-haired, fatherly man who explained Bradley's *Theory of Tragedy* to us and portrayed Shakespeare as the great Moral Teacher recognized by the Victorian age. He read from the plays, modestly skipping the

22

coarser passages which we enjoyed secretly at our desks. Fr. George O'Neill, our Professor of Philology and Language gave us on one occasion the practical task of writing a Petrarchan sonnet, a Spenserian stanza and a short lyric. Thomas MacDonagh liked the lyric which I wrote about a green fantastic valley, and so he invited me to his house.

'A lyric comes suddenly with a lilt or a verbal tune', he exclaimed that day, as soon as we sat down. 'But you may often have to wait for months until the words come'.

Much to my delight he treated me already as a fellow-poet. He talked to me of his favourite lyric writer, Thomas Campion, who was a contemporary of Shakespeare. He was certain that Campion was of Irish descent, for he was described in the minutes of the Parliament held in the Middle Temple in 1565 as 'son and heir of John Campion of Dublin, Ireland, deceased'. The name, formerly pronounced 'Champion' in Ireland and England, was one of the anglicized forms of O'Crowley, in Gaelic, O'Cruaidhlaoch, the grandson of the Head Warrior, or Champion. It is quite common to the present day in Kilkenny and Offaly. Thomas MacDonagh explained to me his own theory of song-verse and speech-verse, quoted from the songs which Campion wrote and set to music, read out a passage from his rich, elaborate prose:

'The Apothecaries have Books of Gold, whose leaves, being opened, are so light, that they are subject to be shaken with the least breath; yet rightly handled, they serve both for ornament and use'.

The small drawing-room was pleasant that afternoon with the fancied sound of lute notes, catches and glees.

As I was leaving, the poet's son, aged about two, toddled out beside us to the kerb. While his father was still talking to me about Tudor lyrics, the child called out as a horse and cart went by 'Look Daddy, at the *capall*!' This was my first experience of the hoped-for bilingual age.

While I was reading for an M.A. degree, I attended the voluntary lectures given by Thomas MacDonagh on Anglo-Irish literature. In these lectures, he explained to us his theory of the Irish Mode, drawing on his study, *Literature in Ireland*, which was published after his execution a year later. As a lecturer he spoke in the easy, lucid, conversational way that shaped the prose of his book. Most of the writers he discussed were new to us and he held us by his enthusiasm. He showed us how translation of poems from Gaelic had led to a new, wavering, delayed rhythm. Thomas Moore had discovered this rhythm when setting words to some Irish folk tunes, as in the lyric which begins:

'At the mid hour of night when stars are weeping I fly'

Callanan used it also in a few of his translations and it was further developed by Samuel Ferguson, for example, in *Cashel of Munster*:

I'd wed you without herds, without money, or rich array,
    And I'd wed you on a dewy morning at day-dawn grey.
My bitter woe it is, love, that we are not far away
    In Cashel town, though the bare deal board were our
        marriage bed this day!

As a young man, Yeats had, with much perception, brought this delayed rhythm back into use:

I will arise and go now, and go to Innisfree.

At a time when many poets still used a stilted diction, Yeats found in native ballads a simple natural speech. MacDonagh was fond of quoting that fascinating lyric from the play *Deirdre*:

'Why is it', Queen Edain said,
'If I do but climb the stair
To the tower overhead,
When the winds are calling there,
Or the gannets calling out
In waste places of the sky,
There's so much to think about
That I cry, that I cry?'

Thomas MacDonagh suggested that I should write a thesis on the influence of lute music in the shaping of the Tudor lyric. For months I picked out Elizabethan tunes on the piano at home, pursued delicate shifts of accent, cunning pauses, wandering, entranced and bewildered, in a region where all was evasive and tantalizingly beyond grasp. As my difficulties increased, I hurried for advice to my tutor and always his enthusiasm sent me away in hope. But when I thought over his words, they were as elusive as the long and short syllables, heavy and light stresses, which tormented my ear.

Once as we were crossing St. Stephen's Green together, Mac Donagh mentioned A.E. 'His mysticism is too vague,' he remarked, comparing it with that of St. John of the Cross. Secretly, I resented what he said, for I admired the poems of A.E., but I kept a respectful silence. On another occasion, thinking of some of my less serious companions in class, I began, with youthful pomposity 'Mr. MacDonagh, why do you cast . . .' Before I could finish, he glanced at me sharply 'Who are the swine?' I was abashed for I realized at that moment how deep was his feeling for our country.

One of Thomas MacDonagh's early books had the Whitmanesque title *Songs of Myself*, but his vanity was so innocent and gay, that it was inoffensive. He told us how he had often gone into the bookshops to enquire about the sales of his books.

'Publish here', he advised me, great was still the reputation of Dublin since the Revival.

Students watch their lecturers with close attention, so it was that late in the Spring of 1916, I began to realize, with a feeling of foreboding, that something was about to happen for I noticed at times, though only for a few seconds, how abstracted and worried Thomas MacDonagh looked. Suddenly, one day, during a lecture on the Young Ireland Poets, he took a large revolver from his pocket and laid it on the desk, 'Ireland can only win freedom by force' he remarked, as if to himself.

The young are conventional and so I was shocked by what he had done. I remembered a story about Edmund Burke, which Professor Donovan had read to us in our First Arts Class when we were studying *Reflections on the French Revolution*, a book kept on the course in order, no doubt, that all undergraduates should become Constitutionalists and faithful followers of the Irish Party at Westminster. During a speech the great orator had flourished and flung a dagger on the floor of the House of Commons, offending members by that histrionic gesture.

Shortly after I had discovered the Abbey, a small theatre was founded in Hardwick Street by Edward Martyn, for the production of realistic and Continental plays. On my first visit to the hall, I saw

25

MacDonagh and Joseph Plunkett, his fellow-poet, in the front row, watching a play by Ibsen. Plunkett, thin, bespectacled, looked as emaciated as the Spanish Saint in his prison cell at Toledo. I longed so much to be in their company that I followed vaguely what was afoot on the stage.

IV

Thomas MacDonagh wrote much more verse than the other two poet-leaders of the Insurrection. His first book *Through the Ivory Gates* was published in 1903. A year later, another collection appeared. He told me once that he had burned all the unsold copies of his early books under a tree in his garden. But after a mediocre start, he slowly developed and his increasing skill owed much to his practice in translating poems from the Irish. Samuel Ferguson was a fine translator but at times he failed. Ernest Boyd has given this example:

> The sun has set, the stars are still,
> The red moon hides behind the hill;
> The tide has left the brown beach bare,
> The birds have left the upper air.

Compare this with the lively movement of the version made by MacDonagh.

> The stars stand up in the air,
> The sun and the moon are gone,
> The strand of its waters is bare,
> And her sway is swept from the swan.

The poet had in fact, a rare gift for translation as is shown by 'The Yellow Bittern' adapted from the mock elegy by Cathal Buidhe Mac Giolla Chumma. The internal rhyme and assonance of the original are echoed in it.

> The yellow bittern that never broke out
>   In a drinking bout, might as well have drunk;
> His bones are thrown on a naked stone

26

Where he lived alone like a hermit monk.
O yellow bittern! I pity your lot,
    Though they say that a sot like myself is curst –
I was sober for a while, but I'll drink and be wise,
    For fear in the end I should die of thirst.

The poems of Thomas MacDonagh are varied in their subject,
ranging from nature, love, patriotism to mysticism.

I was reminded of his poem 'Grange House Lodge' recently,
when I passed by that estate, for the cottage in which the poet had
lived for several years was no longer there. W. B. Yeats admired
some of the poetry of MacDonagh, but critics have not noticed that
he was infuenced by two of them. MacDonagh wrote two poems
for his children. 'Wishes for my son, born on St. Cecilia's Day' and
'Barbara'. Some years later, Yeats wrote 'A Prayer for my
Daughter' and 'A Prayer for my Son'. One of MacDonagh's best
poems is the character study 'John-John', tender and humorous:

I dreamt last night of you, John-John,
    And I thought you called to me:
And when I woke this morning, John,
    Yourself I hoped to see;
But I was all alone, John-John,
    Though still I heard you call,
I put my boots and bonnet on,
    And took my Sunday shawl,
And went, full sure to find you, John,
    To Nenagh fair.

The fair was just the same as then,
    Five years ago today,
When first you left the thimble men
    And came with me away;
For there again were thimble men
    And shooting galleries,
And card trick men and Maggie men
    Of all sorts and degrees, –
But not a sight of you, John-John,
    Was anywhere.

27

Equally original is that neglected poem, 'The Night Hunt', and here is a small poem with a moral, which is apt in these ecumenical times:

Calvin and Chaucer I saw today
Come into the Terenure Car;
Certain I am that it was they,
Though someone may know them here and say
What different men they are.
I know their pictures – and there they sat,
And passing the Catholic Church at Rathgar,
Calvin took off his hat
And blessed himself, and Chaucer at that
Chuckled and looked away.

Four

I

ON THE MORNING of Easter Monday, the road outside our terrace was quiet. Thousands had already left the city on their way to the Fairyhouse Races by train, on outside cars, in traps, wagonettes, and even in Ford cars. My eldest sister, Doto, and I were busy in the sunny breakfast room. She was playing a tune by John Dowland on the piano for me, which I had copied out in the National Library from an old Book of Ayres. Suddenly, the sidedoor bell rang urgently. She hurried to answer the ringing and in less than a minute, my father, mother and Eileen were with us, listening in astonishment as an excited neighbour told us the news.

'The G.P.O. has been occupied by the Volunteers. . . . The tricolour of the Irish Republic is flying above it. . . . Jacob's factory . . . Boland's Mill have also been occupied. . . . Some say there has been an attack on Dublin Castle. . . . The O.T.C. are guarding Trinity College . . . others say all the country is rising . . . the No.10 trams have stopped. . . The Railway Bridge down the road is barricaded'.

We went out to the front gate. A quarter of a mile down the road, we could see a double-decker tram on the Bridge, over the railway line, with upturned carts piled on each side of it.

Another neighbour came to the gate to tell us that a regiment of Lancers had been scattered near Nelson Pillar.

In a couple of minutes, I was among the sightseers at the barricade, my bicycle against the nearby railings. Five or six Volunteers, a couple of them in green uniforms, were on guard, while others were at their posts in the upper windows of several houses on each side of the road, with rifles ready. I noticed with surprise when I looked down the railway line towards Cabra, that the other bridge had not been barricaded. This seemed odd planning and I wondered whether the Lancers had trotted down the Cabra Road to the city.

One of the Volunteers was a medical student from our College, whom I knew well, a large earnest fellow with a slow stammer. He had been called up that morning, but would tell me nothing of what had happened. He was in his ordinary clothes and wore a bandolier. I did not mention anything to him about the other unguarded bridge.

I cycled home to report, and at about half-past twelve passed the barricade again, pedalling as fast as I could by Doyle's Corner, over the Canal Bridge, by Goldsmith Street, the Mater Hospital, down Blessington Street to Rutland Square.

Lower O'Connell Street, to my surprise, was silent and without people. On the left near Nelson Pillar, a dead horse lay on the road – a melancholy sight. When I came nearer, I saw a little crowd outside the General Post Office and the tricolour – green, white and yellow – fluttering above the great building. Inside the sand-bagged windows were armed men, silent, watchful.

I turned to read the printed proclamation on an electric standard at the corner:

> The Republic guarantees religious and civil liberty, equal rights and equal opportunities to all citizens and declares its resolve to pursue the happiness and prosperity of the whole nation and of all its parts, cherishing all the children of the nation equally. . . .

I crossed the street and wheeled my bicycle slowly by the kerb. Within a shop doorway, near the D.B.C., I was alarmed to see a workman, bristled, unshaven, smoking a clay pipe contentedly, as he sat, rifle on knee, I guessed that he was a member of the Citizen Army. Carlyle's description of the Reign of Terror came into my mind: I heard the creaking of the tumbrils, the shouts of the sans-culottes. I went past the O'Connell Monument, feeling ashamed of the middle-class snobbery which had disturbed my patriotic emotion for I thought I had rid myself of it when I left school.

Soon I was among the crowd outside the College of Surgeons in St. Stephen's Green. Behind the sandbagged windows were armed men, silent, watchful. A few people were peering between the railings of the Park and I hurried over to join them. Volunteers were digging trenches across the path inside and I wondered why they were doing so, for it was obvious that they could be shot down mercilessly from the high houses around the Green.

Puzzled and bewildered, I cycled down Grafton Street, past the G.P.O., up Rutland Square, to Phibsborough Church, and soon was at the barricade again. My student friend was not there, and one of the Volunteers told me that he had been sent for, as his father had been taken ill and was dying. He would be back shortly. I wondered why this officer had given him leave. Later I heard what happened. When he got home to Drumcondra, he found that his father was quite well. He was angry at the trick which had been played on him. His mother, however, persuaded him to change into an older suit and while he was doing so, his father locked the bedroom door. After the Rebellion was over, he gave himself up and was interned in the camp at Frongach in Wales.

II

It was about five o'clock in the afternoon when I met Stephen MacKenna in the middle of O'Connell Street, directly opposite the G.P.O. A restless, difficult crowd was gathered at the corner of Earl Street, while a few Volunteers armed with rifles and in full green uniform were endeavouring to keep order. As I made my way here and there through the scattered groups, I saw Stephen MacKenna alone in a little space, lost in thought, indifferent to those about him. He was leaning weakly against a tram standard, but he greeted me in his quick melancholy way. He told me that he had hurried down that morning as soon as he heard the news. He had been there all day. He looked pale and ill: it was obvious that only the intensity of his own feelings and of the event itself had sustained him. The G.P.O. was already cold grey in the shadow and beyond passing heads I could see again, almost obscured by the great pillars, the watchful figures of armed men behind the sand-bagged windows. Clearly against the blue sky above the roof waved the flag of the Irish Republic declared that morning.

Stephen MacKenna said little to me. Thought, emotion, could find no other end for themselves than the words 'At Last'. Certainly, neither of us mentioned any of those friends who, as we knew, must be at their posts, so near to us or somewhere else in the city. The

31

historic hour existed with all its secret, countless memories of the past, in and of itself, so that even the feeling of suspense and of coming disaster seemed to belong to a lesser experience of reality. It is difficult now to recapture that emotion, that thought, from which even the crowd, dimly hostile or, perhaps, taken by total surprise, was scarcely a distraction. It has become quite easy to forget how completely the country had turned away from its own individual, national life, to forget how bitterly the few awakeners and poets who revived pride, were hated and abused.

As I stood silently beside Stephen MacKenna, I was increasingly aware, not only of a supreme event but of the painful emotion in his few broken words from time to time. I was still a student, with a healthy respect both for his Greek scholarship and for the wilful anger which I had once innocently drawn upon myself. His tormented exaltation – which I secretly understood – filled me with a superstitious alarm for him. I wanted to be alone, even to be rid of him, that I might think of Wolfe Tone, Robert Emmet, and the hosts of the dead.

Realising that his wife and others might be already searching for him, and calling to mind the imminent danger in the city, I tried vaguely to persuade him to leave. By then, he had almost forgotten my presence – perhaps, he too, wished to be rid of me. After a few timid, futile efforts, I went away, full of compunction, leaving him to his thoughts.

III

During the week the North Circular Road was quiet. There was no shortage of supplies. The milkman from Finglas measured out the pints of milk every morning at the sidedoor. We could get food at the provision shops in Prussia Street or Manor Street. Rumours were increasing. A gun-boat had steamed up the Liffey to shell Liberty Hall. A regiment of British soldiers marching from Kingstown Harbour into Dublin were ambushed at Mount Street Bridge by snipers in houses, firing across the Canal from Boland's Mill. Tyler's shoeshop and several drapery stores had been looted. Everyone knew the sturdy story of the shawled woman, making her way down Henry Street with a load of stolen goods. A man grabbed them from her and she called indignantly on bystanders, as she rushed after him, bawling 'Stop thief. Stop thief, I've been robbed'.

A lonely little story went its humorous way and then disappeared. An alarmed young sentry on duty near Palmerston Park had asked a passerby – 'Soi, Moite, wen will the troibes kam dahn frome the 'ills?'.

I met the eldest son of Professor Donovan, who had joined the British army. He was home on leave for a few weeks and wore mufti. He told me he had seen Thomas MacDonagh in a car with others driving down Thomas Street from the South Dublin Union which had been taken over by the Rebels. I was depressed by his indifferent tone, but too timid to say anything. Clearly I could see the poet driving past the house where Lord Edward Fitzgerald had been captured, no longer worried, but smiling, grave. All the week, I could see him passing that house on his way back to Jacob's factory and was filled with foreboding.

The barricade at the Railway Bridge had been closed. I could still reach the Quays, however, by way of Grangegorman, which was almost opposite St. Alban's Terrace. I cycled past the high wall of the asylum, went by the distillery at Smithfield on by Queen Street. All the streets were silent, even the hall-doors of the tenement houses were closed. Once as I was standing within the doorway of a public house on the Quays, opposite Watling Street, listening to the volleys across the river, a stray bullet hit the wall above. A few flakes of brick fell. I realized for the first time why everyone in the houses near the Quays did not venture out.

Every evening, my married sister Kathleen, who lived in Glasnevin, made her way by the side-streets to us. Always she was in a state of excitement though she had little to tell. As often as she could, she joined the small crowds of watchers at the corner of Rutland Square, opposite Findlater's Church, retreating hastily with the rest, when the volleys across O'Connell Street seemed too near, pressing forward again during a lull.

One night, on her way home she was stopped with several other people at Binn's Bridge by a party of British soldiers. An elderly woman went on, although a young sentry called to her several times to stop. Before anyone could rush forward to drag her back, he raised his rifle, fired, and she fell dead on the pavement. Afterwards, a girl who had known her told my sister that the old woman had been stone-deaf for many years.

During the struggle for independence, hasty encounters between a score of British soldiers and hedge-hidden guerrilla-fighters were always described largely in the newspapers as battles. So I record now the forgotten Battle of the North Circular Road, in which a regiment fought alone.

On the third sunny day of the Rising, at two o'clock in the afternoon, I was sitting in a deck-chair in the front garden, when I heard a rattle around the bend near our house. I got up and saw the muzzle of a field-gun protruding around the corner. A few soldiers in war-time khaki, accompanied by an officer, were pushing it forward. As they crouched behind its low shield, the gunner took aim. I heard the bang as the shell went by and a few seconds later the crash of it into the tram a quarter of a mile away. Then like the last feeble reverberations of its echo came the crackle of a volley from the houses beside the barricade. Half a dozen shells hurtled by in rapid succession. The carts were blown to smithereens. The tram was still there, gaunt and shattered.

Mr. Bergin, the corn-factor who lived next door and his sister, Mrs. Maughan, a widow with seven annoying cats, were in their front garden like us. No one was alarmed, for in those days of British rule, we were used to the sight of soldiers. Every evening, Tommies in their smart red tunics and dark blue trousers, silver knobbed canes under their arm, strutted towards the city to flirt with girls in Lower O'Connell Street. In the house on our left, the two spinsters were watching from one of the top windows.

Then, around the corner, a regiment of soldiers came, pressing against the wall. Some crept along by the garden railings, others stooped by the flower-beds, and dropped quickly over the low walls. As they filed slowly through our garden, a young soldier stopped to ask Doto for a drink of water. He was trembling, and pitying him she hurried in to get a tumbler-full. As he gulped the water down, I glared at her as boldly as I could, in patriotic indignation. Slowly the soldiers moved from garden to garden or crouched by the railings, then darted from gate to gate. In the silence, there was only the clump of their boots on the pavement, the rattle of their gun-butts. It seemed like a mock advance in manoeuvres. We watched, keeping our secret from the enemy. As there had been only one round of rifle shots from the bridge, we knew that the Volunteers, acting under orders – frightened by the shelling – had skipped over the backgarden walls and fled along the railway embankment.

Soon most of our neighbours left the doorsteps and went back to their sitting-rooms. Even the two old maids had retired from their favourite window. I waited on, watching caps bobbing up and down quickly, bodies slumping over the walls between flowering shrubs, or hunkering along the pavement. The twenty minutes of advance seemed as slow as an hour.

At last, the entire regiment seemed to have vanished. There was a long pause, but I knew that at any moment the attack would start. Suddenly, there was volley after volley. Then a detachment of the infantry charged past the broken barricade. In a few moments, the empty houses had been captured.

The Battle of the North Circular Road was over.

Rumours had ceased. The sunny weather continued and in a few days another leaf would be pulled from the Almanac. Fear was everywhere. All were aware of the approaching might of Great Britain, terrible as that of the Kaiser. Some were waiting for the sea-rumble when our ancient city would be bombarded by warships.

V

Something strange was going on in our house, but I did not pretend to notice it. Then, one night, as I sat in my small study in the return, the door opened. My father brought someone in with him and quickly left us to talk. I was much surprised to find myself greeting an old family friend, an engineer in the Dublin Corporation for I thought that he was in the Pigeon House, the electric power station near Ringsend. I had understood that he was Commandant of the small force that had occupied it on Easter Monday morning.

He was a middle-sized man, about forty years of age, with a dark pointed beard, always full of high spirits, always ready to play another practical joke. Once, when I was much younger, he had given me a fright. The downstairs bell rang at twilight and when I opened the sidedoor, a dwarf rushed past me along the passage. The next moment, I saw the engineer leaning against the wall, laughing

35

at me after his acrobatic act.

But, this night, he was pale, agitated, I guessed that he had failed to turn up at his post. He talked awkwardly to me about my studies, took several books from the shelves and put them back. Every quarter of an hour he left the room hurriedly and went upstairs. While he was in the bathroom I thought of him with contempt, for the young are harsh in their judgement. While I smoked my pipe, poked the fire in the small grate, I wondered what had happened at the Pigeon House.

On the next night, he was back again in my room and, as before, neither of us mentioned the events of the week. Every quarter of an hour, he left the room restlessly and I could hear him going upstairs. I did not see him again after the second night.

At last, rumours came back. Smoke was rising from the centre of the city. The G.P.O., the Gresham Hotel and several large buildings in O'Connell Street were ablaze. Padraic Pearse and the other leaders had surrendered unconditionally. Hundreds of Volunteers were prisoners in the military barracks. Only Eamonn De Valera was holding out with his riflemen in Boland's Mill.

The newspapers were on sale again. Aghast, day after day, we read of the execution of the signatories of the Proclamation, one by one. In the British House of Commons, John Dillon, one of the leading members of the Irish Parliamentary Party, pleaded in vain for clemency.

The *Irish Independent*, the clericalist newspaper owned by William Martin Murphy, the formidable magnate of the Lock Out three years previously, demanded the blood of the Socialist leader, James Connolly, who had been badly wounded.

General Maxwell obeyed what was claimed to be the will of the people. James Connolly was carried out in a chair and shot.

My father had disappeared from the house on a secret journey. Later, I learned that he had smuggled his old friend out of the country to Liverpool. Then, in his affable way, with the help of some bribing, he had got the Commandant, disguised as a stoker, on board a liner leaving for New York.

Exhausted by work in the furnace room, fear and remorse, the unfortunate fugitive died a few weeks later of double pneumonia in an American hospital, leaving, penniless in Dublin, his wife and two small children.

Five

AFTER THE RISING, I realized, despairingly, that it would be a waste of time to continue my thesis on the development of the Tudor and Caroline Lyric. As the work had to be submitted within two months, I had to find another subject. Having read a good deal of Elizabethan drama, I decided to write a study of John Ford, about whom no book had as yet been published. I was attracted to his plays because Maeterlinck had translated *'Tis Pity She's a Whore*. The Belgian poet changed the deliberately cruel title, using, instead, the name of the heroine, Annabelle. The previous year I had fallen in love with a girl student and when all went awry, I remained for several months in a stupor. So the dumb grief in those poetic tragedies drew me and the subtle, melancholic lines beyond the range of Shakespeare, kept repeating themselves in my mind:

> Sigh out a lamentable tale of things
> Done long ago, and ill done: and when sighs
> Are wearied, piece up what remains behind
> With weeping eyes, and hearts that bleed to death.

And again:

> Parthenophil is lost, and I would see him;
> For he is like to something I remember,
> A great while since, a long, long time ago.

My own misery moved to the lute songs within the tiring house:

> O, no more, no more, too late
> Sighs are spent: the burning tapers
> Of a life as chaste as fate,

37

Pure as are unwritten papers,
Are burnt out: no heat, no light
Now remains: 'tis ever night.

As I knew nothing about methods of research, I wrote to W. J.
Lawrence, whose books on the Elizabethan stage I had read, and he
invited me to come and see him. This scholar, who contributed
articles to learned journals in Germany and other countries, had
been a commercial traveller in Belfast before his extraordinary
change. I had heard him asking questions at a few literary meetings:
a thin, grey-haired man, acute, accurate, with a clipped Northern
accent. The top-front room in Haddington Road, where he lived,
was poorly furnished and I was embarrassed by the large
double-bed in a corner of it. His wife, soft, fat and motherly, made
tea for us, and I noticed that they could only afford Condensed Milk.
As I nibbled at a slice of bread and cheap margarine, I hoped that I
was not encroaching on their breakfast.

Having no degree, Lawrence had been unable to obtain an
academic post and his library consisted of a large wooden box,
crammed with notebooks which he had used in the Bodleian, and
the British Museum. By his intensive study, word by word, of the
plays, he had been the first to discover many details about the
structure of the Elizabethan stage, the costumes worn, the
mechanical devices. He had even deduced the prices of admission.
He had a remarkable memory for details and dates. Sometimes he
would rummage for a notebook or bundle of papers in his magic
box. His knowledge of eighteenth-century comedies was as minute,
and I found it hard to keep him from speaking of them. I called to
his lodgings several times, but despite his eagerness to help me, I
profited only from his encouraging words and the example of his
zeal. In his downright, businesslike way, he was concerned with
facts, but had little interest in blank verse and the verbal music of
lyrics.

Soon afterwards, W. J. Lawrence lectured at a number of
universities in the United States. When that country joined the Allies
in the struggle against Germany, he was forced to work for a living
in a munitions factory. On his return, he settled down with his wife
in London and was given a small pension by the British Government
which kept him from destitution. In his last years, he was troubled

38

by prostate gland. Rightly distrusting nature, the worthy man never went out alone in the London streets.

II

It is a notorious fact that a degree in Arts is of little practical value. So when I became an M.A., my only gains were an ornamental scroll of imitation parchment and a photograph of myself in hired cap and gown. I decided to live by music and took up my violin which had been left in its case for five years. After three months of hard practice, I applied for a position of violinist in a New Ross cinema, but, at the ensuing interview, I was rejected. I decided to try journalism and, as it was necessary to know shorthand and typing, I joined a new college in the basement of a commercial building in Dame Street. Mentally it was a bewildering experience even though I had chosen one of the easier systems of stenography because I discovered in a few days that the signs were based on a very crude method of setting down spoken sounds. As the teacher dictated, we listened and wrote down the signs. 'Ought' became 'aut': 'knee' was 'ne' and I puzzled over a word such as 'Jem' wondering whether it represented 'Gem' or 'jam'. As the course advanced, the abbreviations intensified: diphthongs, syllables, consonants, disappeared, and, in the words of Calverley, in his parody of Browning 'we docked the smaller parts of speech and curtailed the already curtailed cur'. We wrote 'prapes' for 'perhaps': to our coarsening ear 'mention' became 'menshun' 'session' was 'seshun'. Before us in the immediate future were ever more dreadful mnemonics – 'nft' for 'indefatigible' and 'krksk' for 'characteristic'. After a couple of months, I found that I could scarcely read a page of prose without translating it in my mind into this jargon and I thought that soon my delight in the vowel music and sound pattern of poetry would be destroyed.

I struggled with dots, dashes, hooks and curves, consoling myself with the thought that the well-known poet, James Cousins, had been a teacher of shorthand in Belfast in his early years and had even edited a Shorthand Journal. His first book of verse was not good and I suspected that its facility was due to his preoccupation with stenography – the conventional words had come so quickly that he must have taken them down in shorthand. I could not help noticing that his poems improved when he gave up teaching and abandoned the *calamo volante*.

Our shorthand teacher in the new college was about thirty-eight, handsome, curly-headed, light of heart, but he preferred to talk rather than to instruct and, being all dunces at dictation, we listened to him in admiration and were glad to do nothing. He had been a newspaper reporter and had gone travelling: indeed he seemed to have been over half the world and the only book which he had read since he left school was his shorthand manual. The less he knew about any subject, the more confidently did he speak about it. Politics, economics, law, medicine, drama, the customs of far-away countries – he dogmatized in his pleasant way about them all. When I showed him a short poem which I had written and typed out as an exercise, he told me what was wrong with it and corrected the lines for me with great affability. I found him fascinating for it was the first time that I had met the complete chancer, the perfect Philistine.

Despite its commercial use in modern times, the invention of shorthand has been attributed to a famous poet of the classical centuries. Quintus Ennius, the first of the Roman poets, wrote a prodigious amount and we may suspect that he evolved a system of shorthand in order to keep pace with the thoughts which thronged through his brain as he scratched them on waxen tablets. It was an alphabetical notation based on words rather than on sounds and so did not distract his Muse. The eighteen books of Annals, the great historical epic written by him, are lost, but, ironically enough, the basic idea of his shorthand survived throughout the Middle Ages.

The Elizbethan dramatists were victims of unscrupulous shorthand writers and were loud in their complaints. Thomas Heywood, in one of his Prologues, mentions the crowds, thronging the seats, the boxes and the stage:

> So much that some by stenographers invent
> A plot, put it in print, scarce one word true.

An eighteenth-century poet, John Biron, was responsible for a considerable improvement in the device of speed-writing. Lord Chesterfield, Walpole and other literary men were among his grown-up pupils. The title of his book was *The Universal English*

Shorthand or the Way of Writing English in the most Easy, Concise, Regular and Beautiful Manner. This suggests that elegance of caligraphy meant as much as speed to the poet. It was only in the age of industrialization that new systems of shorthand replaced the older ones. Numerous rival systems of shorthand in every country have been due to the craze for speed. But no businessman could dictate as many words to the minute as an expert stenographer is capable of setting down.

One morning, when I arrived in class, our teacher was not there. In his place was the Principal of the College, a small, worried man with a Northern accent, who had come in great haste from Belfast. He told us that our good-humoured, easy-going teacher had vanished, taking with him all our fees. So ended abruptly my brief course in shorthand and typing.

Soon afterwards I was appointed Assistant Lecturer in English at U.C.D. Somebody told me that Frank Fay had returned to Dublin to earn his livelihood as a teacher of elocution. So I decided to take a short course with him in correct speaking. As one of the founders of our National Theatre, Frank Fay was a legend to us and already I could hear his wonderful voice as he spoke on the Abbey stage in the plays of Yeats. I was completely surprised therefore, and disappointed when I met him in the lodging house where he was staying. He was a small man, quick in gesture and speech. He told me that he had abandoned the poetic method of his early years and he insisted on the brisk pronunciation used on the English stage. I resisted his abrupt enunciation but one word of his remained in my mouth: I still say mod'n instead of modern. His enthusiasm and method of teaching were remarkable and in a few weeks, after much practice, I had learned to project my voice. I was so moved by his poverty and shabby appearance that I felt ashamed at the end of each lesson as I slipped the pathetic fee of 3s. 6d. into his hand. On the morning of the final lesson he brought me to the Abbey Theatre and listened from the back of the pit as I declaimed Mark Anthony's speech to the mob from Shakespeare's *Julius Caesar*, much embarrassed by the presence of a couple of charwomen with clattering buckets and knocking brooms in the stalls below.

During his first tour of the United States with the other actors and actresses who had left the Abbey Company, Frank Fay wrote embittered letters to a friend in Dublin, in which he attacked Yeats for his mischievous intrigues behind the scenes, and also Lady Gregory. He complained that Synge, being afraid of them, would not intervene.

After the death of his former associate, Yeats seems to have had some stirring of conscience for he added, in expiation, a florid dedication to *The King's Threshold*: 'In Memory of Frank Fay for his beautiful speaking in the character of Senechan'. His magnanimity had come too late.

III

Dr. George Sigerson, who was Professor of Zoology at University College, Dublin, was best known as a Gaelic scholar and pioneer. His large volume of translations *Bards of the Gael and Gall* in the original metres was already old-fashioned, since the poet in his literary version used double rhyme and jingling internal rhyme.

When I met him, he was in his eighties, a stately, portly figure, always dressed in a frock-coat. His mane of white hair gave him a bardic appearance, and with his imperial beard reminded one that he had studied biology in Paris with Charcot long ago and physiology with Claude Bernard. He was proud of his Viking descent and held that Scandinavian plunderers, had been maligned by historians. In this he was probably right for the 'Danes' founded Dublin in the Black Pool of the Liffey and our other sea-towns.

Often as I passed his lecture room, the din of students' voices, shuffling of feet, banging of desks, angered me for I had great reverence for him. Dr. Sigerson, however, ignored the tumult, though at times he made apt and caustic remarks. The students were accustomed to writing down their queries on slips of paper and leaving them on his desk. One day, he picked up a slip with the words 'Silly Ass' scrawled on it. 'Will the student who left his visiting-card, please remain after class', remarked Dr. Sigerson, as he picked it up and adjusted his pince-nez.

At that time I was English Assistant and happened one day to be in the Professors' Room. Dr. Sigerson came in and, looking at me in a curious way, said 'Come and see me next Tuesday at four - o'clock'.

When I came to his house in Clare Street, he gave me treatment with a galvanic battery. Wonderingly, I clutched the brass handles and endured the mild shocks. He told me to come for a regular course and also ordered me to eat black puddings because of their wholesomencss. He asked me to dinner on several occasions. These were formal and the male guests in turn offered an arm to the ladies and accompanied them gravely to the dining-room.

Like many Dublin doctors, Sigerson was a collector and specialized in Napoleonic and other miniatures. Once he brought me into a long dusty room crammed with ornate tables, sideboards, gilt mirrors. It resembled an auction room or secondhand furniture shop.

One evening he told me of an experience in a remote district of the south. A young man was suffering from the 'mountain gloom' and for several years had lain abed. Dr. Sigerson conspired with his father and brothers. They put the tip of a ploughshare in the fire until it was red-hot. Then at a given signal the men whipped off the bed clothes and turning the wretched youth on his face, they pulled up his night-shirt. Expertly the doctor touched his coccyx with the red-hot tip. Uttering shrieks, the young fellow leaped from the bed, and disappeared from the house. In a few hours, he returned, completely cured.

Dr. Sigerson regarded with mild contempt the Celtic Twilight movement and in his dry Northern accent often spoke of it to me. Once he told me of an encounter with W. B. Yeats in his carly years. It was on a sunny Saturday morning in his surgery and someone had brought with him a crystal. Yeats placed it on a small table near the window and gazed into it.

'I see a cloud', he chanted, 'It is parting slowly . . . and now I can see a stately figure . . . in white robcs waving his arms. He is wearing a gold crown . . . beyond him are other figures in purple, green and gold'. . . . 'If you look out of the window', dryly remarked Dr. Sigerson, 'you will notice a Medical Hall on the opposite side of the street. A man in white overalls is cleaning the brasses and on the top shelf of the shop-window, are large glass vessels with purple, green and yellow liquid in them – pharmaceutical emblems'.

I attended for a month. Unfortunately, neither the pins-and-needles of the galvanic battery nor the black puddings saved me from collapse in a few months, because there is no cure for the folly of youth or the dire consequences of overindulgence in continence.

So every evening, I hurried across the city to see Margaret who lived in a flat in one of the tall Victorian houses in Lower Pembroke Street. Usually, we had a collation: cold chicken and a cheap bottle of Australian wine. Later she lit two candles, and switched off the electric light. By the glow of the fire under a painting of Byzantine domes, she became more mysterious. She had spent some years in Vienna but I knew little of her past, except from one of her poems in which she hinted that an Austrian officer had committed suicide because of her. This, however, seemed to me only a romantic wish. When the street below was silent, she retired to her small bedroom for a few minutes and then came back in her night-dress, her black tresses flowing almost to her knees.

Was I the last young poet to lie under such heaviness of hair, while I clasped her in my arms? Dimly I suspected her secret, when, in her passionate self-struggle, like Telisiphe, Attlis or Mergara, she forgot long after midnight that I was with her.

Six

DURING THE REVOLUTIONARY YEARS, Auxiliaries, Black and Tans, drove through the capital in armoured cars and wire-netted lorries. It was a time of alarms, constant incursions, street explosions, sudden haltings at barriers.

One day, I called at noon to see F. R. Higgins in his office near Nelson Pillar, where he edited *The Shamrock*. This weekly periodical had been bought by Alderman Farrell, owner of several cinemas. To the delight of elderly readers, Higgins had revived a serial, popular in Victorian times, which dealt with the comic adventures of a character called Mick McQuaid.

We left the office and went around the corner to the Tower Bar in Henry Street. There were only a couple of other drinkers there. We stood at the counter chatting and then Higgins passed me the proof of a short poem which I had given him, a youthful and rather rude satire addressed to our senior, James Stephens. While I was correcting it, I was aware vaguely of men crowding into the bar and then I felt someone elbowing me in the ribs. I moved slightly but the nudging went on. I was about to turn angrily when I heard, at what seemed a great distance, the quivering voice of Higgins: 'Clarke, Clarke, put up your hands!'

I turned and saw my friend with his hands above his big hat, completely surrounded by formidable men in raincoats, and glancing down, found that a large Colt revolver held by a squat, grim fellow was pressing my side. I promptly put up my hands so that he might search me. With a look of distaste, the stranger put back in my vest pocket the large watch which had cost three-and-sixpence, and then began to read the bundle of letters he took from my breast-pocket. A pleasant-looking young officer in uniform appeared and I protested to him indignantly that his man was reading private love-letters of mine. He smiled, told the Black and Tan to give them back to me – and so the search was over. But Higgins went through a bad time, for his capacious pockets were bulging with the galleys which he was bringing down to the printers. After ten minutes nothing seditious was found in the 'pulls'. As we left the public-house, we saw to our surprise that a large crowd had gathered outside. Instantly it divided, and chatting nonchantly, we sauntered past the admiring throng until we got around the corner where we burst out laughing. For twenty seconds we had felt the thrill which Eamonn De Valera, Sean Lemass and other heroes had known so often.

A few weeks later, Alderman Farrell came with an article of his own to his young editor. It was an attack on a fellow member of the Corporation. Higgins hurried with it shrewdly to a solicitor, who told him that it contained criminal libel. The Alderman gave up the periodical and Higgins had to found another trade-paper.

II

Shortly after this, I happened to feel one night, when undressing, a small hard object under the watch in my waistcoat pocket. It was a revolver bullet. Some months before on my way back from Paris, I had met a young Frenchman who was travelling to Dublin on business. He took out a small automatic pistol and ejecting half a dozen bullets, was about to throw them from the window. It seemed to me a waste of good ammunition and, stirred by patriotic impulse, I asked him to give them to me, for I had bought a pistol of the same calibre when I was in Paris. Had the Black and Tan found that bullet under my watch, I have no doubt that my explanation would neither have been excusable nor credible. With a shiver, I remembered how many prisoners had been shot when trying to escape.

III

In those dire times, it was easy to forget the curfew hour, for no tocsins sounded throughout the city. My home was at Killiney and once, when I wanted to remain the night in town, I arranged with Higgins to stay with him at his lodgings in a side-street near Amiens

Street Railway Station. I was delayed and at about 11 o'clock set out confidently, then realized that I had forgotten the precise directions which the poet had given me. I wandered along the empty streets with scarcely a light showing, except an occasional glimmer through the chinks of a shutter. As I strayed anxiously up Gloucester Street, I met a drunken labourer staggering along the wide pavement. 'Eff the effing Black and Tans!', he shouted.

He stopped from time to time clenching his fist, shouting his foolish defence. Coming up with him, I tried to pacify him and find out from him the street for which I was looking, but my question could not reach him through the whirl of pints. I tried to get him to go home but he still kept defying the foes of his country.

I waited in the shadows until his voice was lost in the distance. I had ten shillings in silver, enough to buy refuge in Night-town, and was tempted by the glow in my thoughts. I resisted it and moved on cautiously.

I had reached Amiens Street. Far away along the road, I heard the hum of a lorry. As I pressed against a doorway, the lorry, full of soldiers, sped by at high speed, glittering with bayonets. I had scarcely gone another hundred yards when I heard the same fearsome sound. Two more lorries, filled with soldiers, rattled by. At last, wandering around side-streets, I came to the house for which I had been searching and knocked timidly at the door. I heard footsteps on the stairs. The landlord, who was a schoolteacher, asked who was there, in as timid a tone as mine. I explained but he refused to open the door. I pleaded through the letter-box, telling him of the danger in which I was at midnight. Suspecting, no doubt, that I was a wanted man, he refused to let me in. I came back to Amiens Street and saw near the Railway Terminus, the glow of a brazier. A watchman and his friend were sitting there in the hut behind the row of lanterns. 'You might get into the Northern Star over there across the road,' said the Watchman. 'If not, you can stay here'. I crossed the road, rang the night bell. In a few moments, the Porter unlocked the gates. I stepped into safety.

A minute later I was in a back-bedroom and soon fell into an uneasy slumber, broken by the noise of goods trains, passing over the viaduct or shunting outside the sheds. Suddenly, in a dream, I saw Margaret in her night-dress once more, pale-faced, her long black tresses let down beyond her waist. I clasped her so

47

passionately, my mouth on hers, that I woke up in feverish desire. So intense was the vision that my mind was made up at last. On the next night, I hurried to her flat just before curfew and asked her to be my wife.

Seven

I

'I KNEW SIR SAMUEL FERGUSON and was often his guest, but knew him only as a kind, courteous and hospitable gentleman: no one ever told me that he was a great Irish Poet'. So Standish O'Grady wrote in an autobiographical fragment entitled *A Wet Day*, which was published in *The Irish Homestead* in 1899. At the time when he met the epic poet, O'Grady was a young Trinity graduate and barrister. He, too, was destined to work without sympathy or recognition, completely unknown to the critics of Victorian England, a hidden pioneer in our own Dark Age. His discovery that his own country had a remote heroic era was sudden and due to chance. While staying with some friends in the West, he happened, on a rainy day, to take a book from the library shelves and glance idly through it. The book was O'Halloran's *History of Ireland* and soon he began to turn the pages in fascinated wonder. The imaginative conversion of O'Grady was so remarkable that we may suspect the ancient bardic associations of his family were astir instinctively in his mind.

It is largely due to the enthusiasm, the unfailing patience, of A.E. that Standish James O'Grady, during the later years of his life, was recognized as the 'Father of the Irish Literary Revival'. He was born in Castletown, Berehaven, in the year 1846, but it is significant that the centenary of his birth should have passed unnoticed and that no public tribute was paid to his name.

Many of us, when we were starting to write, had heard only vaguely of Standish O'Grady, and he was little more to us than a shadowy figure surviving from the past. We knew that he had been living for many years in complete retirement in the Isle of Wight, and had been granted one of those paltry Civil List pensions which the British Government gives with mocking hand. There were rumours that he had outlived his own enthusiasm, forgotten the epic mood of his early years. Most of his books had never been republished and we had never seen any of them. To make matters worse, it was easy to confuse his name with that of another Irish scholar, his cousin, Standish Hayes O'Grady. Moreover, the latter had also something of the bardic impulse and in *Silva Gadelica*, which inspired Herbert Trench to write *Deirdre Wed*, had fashioned for himself an exuberent, strange prose – equally neglected.

My own acquaintance with the work of O'Grady was sudden, completely unexpected. One Sunday evening when all the guests had gone, I lingered on in A.E's. 'little painted room' as Francis Ledwidge called it in one of his poems. As if glad to be rid of politics and the Ulster question, A.E. began to talk to me about O'Grady, rapidly, excitedly, until the very room became legendary. He moved up and down through a haze of tobacco smoke, quoting long passages from memory, and as I smoked my pipe furiously, hot-mouthed, I could catch glimpses over his shoulder of his own mythological pictures on the walls. Snatching *The History Ireland: Critical and Historical*, the two volumes of *The Bardic History*, he declaimed:

'But all around, in surging, tumultuous motion, come and go the gorgeous, unearthly beings that long ago emanated from bardic minds, a most weird and mocking world. Faces rush out of the darkness, and as swiftly retreat again. Heroes expand into giants and dwindle into goblins or fling aside their heroic form and gamble as buffoons; gorgeous palaces are blown asunder like smoke wreaths; Kings with wands of silver and ard roth of gold, move with all their state from century to century; puissant heroes, whose fame reverberates through battles, are shifted from place to place . . . buried monarchs reappear. The explorer visits an enchanted land where he is mocked and deluded. Everything is blown loose from its fastenings. All that should be most stable is whirled round and borne away like foam or clear leaves in a storm'.

Even the footnotes were gigantesque. So he wrote of that saga *The Destruction of the Hostel of Da-derga* in which the gods appeared for the last time, three miles away from the river-corner where I live now:

'This great tale starts, in its native weirdness and horror, straight from the heart of the barbaric ages. On every side it opens chasms and weird vistas of thought and feeling, which we cannot now

50

realise or understand.'

After a wild search, A.E. found the later romance *The Flight of the Eagle*. This story of Elizabethan Ireland culminates in a wonderful scene. Red Hugh O'Donnell, on his escape from Wicklow to the North, climbs to the tarn on Slieve Gullion and sees in a vision all the heroic and mythological past.

As I heard for the first time that Homeric roll-call of names, so long forgotten, so lost in our historic night, I was aware for the first time of an older religion than the one I had known from childhood.

Long after midnight, I hurried down Clanbrassil Street and across the Liffey Bridge at Winetavern Street and past the Four Courts, with a thousand years under my arm, for A.E. had lent me those rare, precious volumes. Truth to tell, I was disappointed by those prose elaborations of the sagas when I read them. In their rhetorical style, they belonged to another generation and I had opened them too late. But I understood the imaginative excitement as of shadowy palimpsests, which they aroused in the mind of A.E. in those far-off, hidden, years of his youth.

II

By this time, I was a regular visitor to A.E's gatherings on Sunday nights. Early in the Spring of 1917 I had written a narrative poem on the legend of Diarmuid and Grainne in about six or eight weeks, working every morning in a state of recurrent imaginative excitement. When I had completed the poem, I showed it to Stephen MacKenna. He suggested that I should send it to Ernest Boyd, author of *Ireland's Literary Renaissance*, who was then regarded as the leading Dublin critic. Boyd would not hazard an opinion, but, in turn, advised me to send it to A.E. I did so, and almost at once, came a flattering letter from him. He had given it to Messrs. Maunsel and in a few weeks, I went to their publishing firm in Lower Baggot Street to sign the contract. The manager George Roberts, a small, red-bearded Ulsterman, excitable and grinning, introduced me to the directors, J. M. Hone, thin, pale and remote, and Edward Lysaght, who had written *Irish Eclopues* on his farm in County Clare.

Soon afterwards, I realized that A.E. was a stern moralist. One afternoon, I happened to meet him in St. Stephen's Green as I was coming from University College. Suddenly he stopped on the path near the statue of George IV – which was blown up later – and looking down severely, asked me: 'Did you suggest to George Roberts that he should quote from the letter I sent you on the wrapper of your book?' My surprise and indignation were so obvious that A.E. laid his hand on my shoulder, beaming down at me like a loving father.

There was the same rite of courtesy every Sunday evening at 17 Rathgar Avenue. The heavy Victorian door, already ajar, creaked on its hinges as friend or stranger arrived. A.E. left the crowded backroom and hurried through the dim-lit hall to welcome the latest arrival: with his great beard, mysterious yet twinkling glance through his glasses, his hair in a glib over his broad forehead. He stood waiting, smiling, while the newcomer put his overcoat and hat on the piled hall-table.

Among the regular guests were James Stephens, Ernest Boyd and his French wife, Madeleine, Constantine Curran who had written about Italian decorators in eighteenth-century Dublin, Professor Osborne Bergin, caustic Gaelic grammarian and poet, Joseph O'Neill, the novelist, and his wife Mary Davenport, George Moore's friend, John Eglington, the portrait-painter, Sarah Purser, a witty and redoubtable spinster. F. R. Higgins told me that he had once met Francis Ledwidge there. The young Meath poet confided to him that he earned £200 a year by writing serials for Boys' Papers in London, but Higgins found this hard to believe. Once, as we were leaving, I met, on the steps, a small, chubby-faced man with a flowing black tie as large as my own. He was James Cousins, the theosophical poet, back on a visit from India.

Every writer or critic who came to Dublin was sure to find his or her way to this Sunday night gathering. Often American women came and, before they spoke, we recognized them by their finely pointed shoes. Inevitably, they asked A.E. about the Fairies, and, with the same patience as Yeats, he explained to them the mysterious orders of the Invisible Ireland. As we knew the disquisition only too well, the rest of us, on such occasions, talked quietly together on the low bench along the wall near the chimney-piece.

Sometimes, I stole a glance at the unlit front room, for the folding doors were kept open: always there was an unfinished canvas on the easel, visual Donegal stacked in the corners. One week night, a young artist, Patrick Tuohy, whose expressive portrait of Joyce's hard-drinking father is well-known, was shown them by A.E. 'Awful!' 'Worse!', exclaimed Tuohy as the poet displayed the canvasses. A.E. continued to hold each up in turn, humble and obedient as a packman.

Everyone talked, smoked, argued – mostly about politics – until ten o'clock, when Violet Russell, helped usually by her two sons, brought in tea. A.E. stood nearby, helpless and smiling, holding a large plate of home-made scones. After tea, as if by pre-arranged signal, Mrs. Russell would call across the room to her husband where he sat waiting in his shabby armchair:

'George, what were you saying to me yesterday about Mr. Asquith?'

or

'George, you mentioned during the week that Sir Edward Carson . . .'

All were silent as A.E. began a monologue which lasted until eleven o'clock. If any visitor ventured to question or contradict him, he brushed aside the rash remark as if it were an annoying fly.

Often, early in the evening, when there were only a few visitors present, A.E. would praise our poems to them and quote entire passages, for he had an amazing memory and could retain in it anything he liked, after he had read it once or twice. 'I am only an extinct volcano', he would explain, leaning back in his armchair with a smile.

The young poets – F. R. Higgins, Monk Gibbon, Lyle Donaghy or myself – each would sit there in happy embarrassment, feeling that he was rumble and fire within, sparks and smoke without.

Late in the evening, when the guests had gone, one or other of us would linger on. As if happy to forget politics and the revolutionary struggle, A.E. would light his pipe again and settle down to talk about poetry. Often he urged us to follow the example of that neglected poet, William Larminie, who was the first to use assonance in a deliberate way, basing his experiments on Gaelic Prosody. In an article published in *The Contemporary Review*, in November 1894, called 'The Development of English Metres' he had expressed ideas which failed to attract attention. Robert Farren, in his book *The Course of Irish Verse* cites the final, ironic passage:

It is true there is a branch of English-writing poets who might be supposed anxious to take the hint. Irish writers would certainly have left their mark upon English literature should they be found to have taken a conspicuous part in the creation of a body of metres, having in them the promise of the future, rich with unexhausted possibilities. But it is to be feared that in spite of much that might lead one to form an opposite anticipation, Irishmen are indisposed to present their ideas to the world in any but the latest, the most fashionable English garb. Therefore, perhaps, Englishmen, who have more self-confidence, will make experiments to encourage them. Should the experiment fail, my countrymen will have been spared the trouble of a fruitless effort, in the event of success, they can then, how much less laboriously, follow in the beaten track.

A.E. would quote from the 'Epilogue to Fand' with its fascinating half-music:

Is there one desires to hear
If within the shores of Eire,
Eyes may still behold the scene
Fair from Fand's enticements?

Let him seek the southern hills
And those lakes of loveliest water
Where the richest blooms of spring
Burn to reddest Autumn;
And the clearest echo sings
Notes a goddess taught her.

Yeats had complained in his *Autobiographies* that he was ill-spoken of in A.E.'s circle, but I never heard him mentioned without respect. A.E. was indeed disappointed by *Reveries over Childhood and Boyhood*, so intensely had he brooded over the early years of his friends. He never referred to his own first visions or to the dreary apprenticeship he had served as an ill-paid clerk in Pims, the haberdashery shop in South Great George's Street. He preferred

54

to share the dreams of that western youth whom he had met in the Dublin School of Art. He quoted long passages from plays and lyrics which were never reprinted. He told us of *The Shadowy Waters*, how, year after year, when Yeats brought him yet another version, the sea-light and mysteriousness seemed less. He pointed out how even in his early lyrics, the young poet was subjective and dimly aware of the duality in his own existence. So he wrote in 'The Indian to his Love':

> A parrot swaying on a tree
> Raging at its own image in the enamelled sea.

and in 'The Sad Shepherd':

> Naught they heard, for they were ever listening,
> The dewdrops, to the sound of their own dropping.

Sometimes, to prove his own theory, A.E. drew from rejected pieces:
> Never with us where the wild fowl chases
> Its shadow along in the evening blaze.
or
> The boy who chases lizards in the grass,
> The sage who deep in central nature delves,
> The preacher waiting the ill hour to pass,
> All these are souls who fly from their dread selves.

Years later, A.E. told me mournfully of his early quarrel with Yeats. George Moore had worked out a plot for that unlucky prose play *Where There is Nothing* and asked Yeats to collaborate with him in the writing of it. Padraic Colum has told me the chief character in it was based on the eccentric religious poet, Philip Francis Little, who had denounced A.E. as a heretic. The collaborators failed to agree and both came with their grievances to A.E., who endeavoured to make peace between them. Before he could do so, Yeats persuaded Arthur Griffith, Editor of *Sinn Féin*, to publish his version in order that he might secure copyright. The play was printed in a special supplement, much to the surprise of A.E. who was disturbed by this display of rustic cunning. As a result

55

their friendship gradually dwindled.

When A.E. spoke of the mystical claims of Yeats, he could not resist mocking them gently. On one occasion he had met him hurrying along Pembroke Road, his olive complexion turned to a bilious green. He had just been present in a nearby house where an Englishman, adept in the Black Art, had sacrificed a cock. The sensitive poet rushed out into the street, horror-stricken by the bloody rite, and never again had anything to do with this ancient cult.

One Sunday, I called to see A.E. in the afternoon. As we talked, in the backroom, lined with books, I looked around occasionally at those early pastels and paintings in which he had depicted in luminous hues the figures of Eastern gods and astral beings, while his conversation ranged from our own myths to Plato's *The Banquet* and the *Vedas*. He told me of the imaginative exercises which Yeats and he were accustomed to practise by concentrating on certain images. Happening to glance out of the window, I noticed that the Dublin Hills were unusually blue in the distance. I looked and saw against them a great shining Being like one of those shown on the walls. After an uneasy minute, still hypnotized by the words of A.E. I turned quickly. The optical illusion was still there. After that I always avoided that window which looked out into the abyss of Los and Orc.

III

On an afternoon in Maytime, I walked with A.E. along the straight road from Rathgar to Templeogue, past the high wall behind which John Eglington, the essayist, lived in a discreet villa. I was proud of my first walk with the great man and hoped that some of my friends would see us together. We called on Professor Heuston, the bacteriologist, at his small early Victorian house beside the Templeogue Bridge, then went down the garden past the lawn, overshadowed by Scotch firs to the river-gate. We wandered along the bank for a short distance by willows. Suddenly A.E. stopped and said 'Look!'

Immediately I stared up at the primrose moon above us. As A.E. followed my glance, I saw under his great beard, paler than lilac, a soft silk bow which once had been purple. 'I wanted to see whether you were subjective or objective'.

He pointed to an ancient May tree, heavy with blossom, which I had not noticed. The dear man gazed at me speculatively, beaming through his lenses in his fatherly way.

IV

'It's like going up to see God,' exclaimed Walter de La Mare as he climbed the six or seven flights of stairs in Plunkett House to the office where A.E. edited *The Irish Statesman*. The first time that I had gone up them was during the years of The Irish Homestead, an agricultural periodical, in which an occasional poem appeared. When I entered the room, A.E. motioned me to a chair. A small countrywoman dressed in tweed, a large basket beside her, was talking to him. I could hear her rustic accent as she went on – 'dis', 'dat', and 'dose'. I assumed that she was a farmer's wife come up to town to seek advice about butter and eggs or some local problem of the Cooperative Movement. So, as I waited, I glanced at the desk, piled high with papers and reference books, the cabinet files behind which I could see parts of the murals of gods and astral figures painted by A.E., their rich hues dimmed by time. As soon as the farmer's wife stopped for a moment, A.E. introduced me to her: 'This is Lady Gregory'.

I was astonished, for I had not recognized her, though I had often seen her head in the front stalls at the Abbey Theatre against the stage-light. Lady Gregory gave a stiff little bow and said shortly: 'We've met before'. No doubt, she had mistaken me for someone else, because she turned away and once more went on with her interminable 'dis', 'dat', and 'dose'. I sat there trying to make out the figures of celestial beings half-hidden by the cabinet files. At last, Lady Gregory picked up her basket, said goodbye to A.E. and, without taking any further notice of me, walked out almost before he had time to open the door for her.

As a young writer, I resented such provinciality. Only later did I realize the remarkable achievement of Lady Gregory. She started her literary career at the age of fifty and published about thirty books – plays, collections of folklores, adaptations of Gaelic epic and legend, essay, reminiscences and diaries.

57

Only once did I see A.E. lose his oriental calm and it was my fault. On a brief visit from London, during the late 'Twenties, I had called to see him at his office. It was on a Thursday afternoon, about four o'clock, when Father Finlay and other Catholic sympathizers with the Co-operative Movement were accustomed to meet there. The clerical agitation for Literary Censorship had been increasing and a few friends were discussing the question, looking like conspirators as they sipped their tea. Among those present were A.E.'s secretary, the poet and wit, Susan Mitchell, Dr. Walter Starkie, George O'Brien, the economist, Senator Michael Tierney, Professor of Greek at University College. Yeats had just published an outspoken attack on the proposed Censorship Bill in *The Spectator* which all praised.

'The fight ought to be carried on in this country,' I exclaimed, 'Why should we always keep running back to stepmother with our troubles?'

A.E. got up with the tea-tray and hurried into the small pantry on the opposite side of the room. I knew by the rattle of the tea cups that he was in a mighty rage. I lingered on after the others had left, trying vainly to explain my point of view, but A.E. remained silent. Later, I kept up with his rapid steps, like an importunate beggar, as he turned the corner of Merrion Row. Halfway up Harcourt Street he stopped to wait for the 15 tram, still silent. When one came, he jumped on, and catching hold of the brass rail, called out to me: 'If you talk like that, you'll be praised in the *Independent*'.

It was a deft blow, for that newspaper, as I have mentioned before, demanded the execution of the wounded leader of the Citizen Army and General Maxwell satisfied the blood-lust of the merciless Catholic Capitalist, William Martin Murphy.

Only later did I realize how powerful were the forces of ex-Republican obscurantism which were behind the demand for Literary Censorship, the hatred of Liberal opinion. Professor Tierney, who spoke with Yeats and a few others in the Senate against the Bill, was assailed so ferociously in the Catholic press that he had to retire from political life.

Although the *Irish Statesman* had only a small weekly circulation, its Editor was regarded with increasing suspicion, because its columns were open to the expression of every kind of opinion. Seumas Clandillon, a former Director of Radio Éireann, published a large collection of folksongs with a vainglorious Introduction and footnotes. In listing a number of inaccuracies, a reviewer in the *Irish Statesman* used some incautious phrases and the insulted collector took a libel action. There was 'a sound of revelry by night' when the only Irish Liberal periodical had to close down owing to the expenees of the case. Attacks on A.E. became more impatient for the Cooperative Movement was contrary to the new policy of uncontrolled private enterprise, industries protected by tariffs, which yielded quick fortunes from home goods ranging from sweets to electric bulbs. During the 'Troubles' the Black and Tans had burned down many creameries throughout the country, but Sir Horace Plunkett and A.E. continued their propaganda. In *The National Being* A.E. expressed the ideal of a Co-operative State and his pen was still busy.

Seán O'Faoláin and other novelists have depicted A.E. in his last few months in Dublin, sitting alone in his backroom on Sunday nights, waiting for the hinges of the halldoor to creak. This is, I think, an exaggeration. Undoubtedly a number of contributors to the *Irish Statesman* went instead to the rival Monday Night held by W. B. Yeats, after the periodical had ceased publication. Moreover, some of the faithful hesitated to call every Sunday night, after the death of A.E.'s wife. They feared to embarrass the poet, for he had none to cook the scones downstairs in the kitchen or to make the tea at ten o'clock. Several friends did their best to find a service flat for him at a reasonable rent but failed. So, A.E. decided to go to London for some time. He looked forward to the change and to the opportunity of meeting old friends. He felt free at last, for he had rid himself of his furniture and temporal effects, and given away all his books.

VII

When A.E. was in London, I came up several times from Bricketwood in Hertfordshire to see him. On the first occasion, while we were having a modest lunch at a restaurant in Oxford Street, he told me confidentially that he had saved enough money from his Lecture Tour in the United States to keep him in his later years. After coffee, we strolled down Regent Street past Eros in Piccadilly Circus to Leicester Square and sat down on a park bench in the spring sunshine as near as we could to the statue of Shakespeare.

'What month were you born in?' he asked me, unexpectedly. 'In May.' He considered for a few moments and then glanced at me several times, his head sideways, as if he were making a rapid crayon sketch.

'As a poet you should wear the moon colours, soft greys, a purple bow or tie and grow a beard.' Somehow, I could not help being shocked. I remembered the innocent remark made by Gerard Manley Hopkins to his fellow-convert, Coventry Patmore, when that uxorious poet showed him the treatise on erotic mysticism, which he had written after his fourth marriage, 'This is telling secrets'.

VIII

Dr. Russell – I stared in surprise at the small brass plate before I pressed the lowest bell in the row beside the halldoor of the drab house in a side-street near Euston. It seemed strange that A.E. should use one of those honorary doctorates which are given so freely and so quickly forgotten. He greeted me happily for he had just been to see an old acquaintance – G. B. Shaw. Better still, a wealthy friend had given him an expensive translation of the *Vedas*. He quoted from them, as if they had excited his imagination again after long years of political controversy and for an hour, the street outside was as remote from me as the Marduk Parade in Babylon, with its rows of statues.

On my next visit, a few weeks later, I had scarcely sat down when A.E. began: 'Are you interested in Shakespeare's sonnets.' 'Not very much though I think that Wilde's theory in *The Portrait of Mr. W.H.* is probably the right one. I've always fancied that it was this essay which brought him under suspicion for the first time'.

A.E. was too excited over his own solution of the riddle to heed what I was saying. He took up a manuscript and read me out his new poem *The Dark Lady*. This long narrative is, I think, the best

60

of his later poems. It begins in the middle of itself – with dramatic abruptness:

> O, no, I was not wanton with that man.
> But to his imagination, yes. I made
> Myself a hundred natures. It is writ,
> My myriad girlhood, in that printed page.
> Or was it I? Did I but play the part
> His magic plotted for me? Did he know
> That his imaginations lived in me
> And swayed me to be one of their own kind,
> To act the bawd for whom an emperor
> Might cast his world away: or it might be
> A maid to whom the world has never come,
> All-innocent upon a fairy isle?
> Yet at the court of the great queen I had
> But one disdainful face, however many
> Wild hearts might beat within me: and high lords
> And Admirals, who had wrecked Armadas, were
> Wrecked on a flinty look. O, I remember.
> My heart swoons to think upon that hour,
> When a young learned gentleman, his head
> Dizzy with gaudy words that had caught fire
> From sun and moon, importuned me to know
> The latest prince of speech.

About a month later, I saw A.E. for the last time. As I came into his room, a quiet man of about forty was leaving. 'He sent me some of his poems. He is a good poet – in the English academic tradition.' The next minute we had left Euston and were back in literary Dublin. While we were talking, A.E. took several spoonfuls from a jar beside him on a small table. He explained that it was Chinese Clay and had been ordered by his doctor. He was sitting with his back to the high Victorian window and as the chill evening sunlight shone on him, I noticed for the first time that he had changed. His face seemed longer, his cheeks were hollowed, his beard was more pointed. He bore a curious likeness to the emaciated Tennyson in his last years. He must have become aware of my anxiety for he told me that he had not long to live. 'Death will be an exciting adventure', he added with a smile.

My thoughts shivered. When he said farewell, I hurried down the street to the nearest post office and sent an urgent telegram to Seumas O'Sullivan. He got in touch with relatives in Hampstead, who brought A.E. to a private nursing-home at Bournemouth. In a week or two, he was dead.

IX

Sean O'Casey was frequently blamed for his attacks on Ultra-montanism in Ireland. Nevertheless, his watchful reading of local newspapers and his strong protests were justified. The new Penal Age had begun. During the late 'Twenties and 'Thirties Catholic Action spread rapidly and the religious minority was impugned as non-Catholic. The names and addresses of all Freemasons were published threateningly in a Catholic periodical. Much, also, was done to widen the differences between North and South because the tariffs were bringing quick fortunes to industrialists. Inflamed by a sermon given in the Jesuit Church, at Gardiner Street, a Dublin mob marched through the streets to Liberty Hall, the Labour Headquarters, singing 'Faith of our Fathers'. As the leaders rushed up steps and stairs, a few men and women escaping by the skylight, crawled in terror along the neighbouring roofs. Sometime later, a group of young Leftists, not more than twenty in number, were denounced weekly in a religious newspaper. Old women and children knelt in prayer on the pavement outside the railings of the basement in which the offenders held their meetings.

The National temper worsened when Senator MacCarthy, the Irish-American lawyer, started his campaign in the United States. As it was quite evident that Ireland was safe from Communistic influence, attention was gradually diverted to Irish poets and novelists. Urged by its most vehement member, James Joyce, an elderly citizen, who had a fanatical dislike of his great namesake, the Censorship Board became as ferocious as that in Spain or Russia. Books by George Moore, Sean O'Casey, Liam O'Flaherty, Con O'Leary, Seán O'Faoláin, Frank O'Connor, myself and others were banned. *The Green Lion*, an autobiographical novel of

Kilkenny, by Francis Hackett, was placed on the prohibited list for its 'obscenity' because of a single, outspoken paragraph. Ecclesiastical pressure increased, when the late Fr. Joseph Deery, parish priest of Mount Merrion was appointed Chairman of the Board. Stricture reached a point that seemed scarcely sane. Kate O'Brien's fine novel *Land of Spices* was banned for a single sentence.

There was consternation in Cork when Christian Brothers discovered in a school anthology on sale in a local book-shop a 'Protestant insult' to Our Lady:

> Joseph and Mary walked
> Through an orchard green
> Where was berries and cherries
> As thick as might be seen.
>
> O then bespoke Mary
> So meek and so mild
> 'Pluck me one cherry Joseph,
> For I am with child'.
>
> O then bespoke Joseph
> With words so unkind
> 'Let him pluck thee a cherry,
> That brought thee with child'.

A.E. pointed out with wry amusement in the *Irish Statesman* that this was one of the famous Cherry Tree carols, composed in the Middle Ages. Unabashed, Ignorance retired to its smoky cell.

F. R. Higgins, after his appointment as Manager of the Abbey Theatre, toured the United States with the first company of players. Shortly after his return he suffered from a stroke. The last months of his life were darkened by virulent attacks in the religious press. He had offered yet another Protestant insult – to the Holy Sacrifice of the Mass. This occurred in the last stanza of a poem in his collection *The Gap of Brightness*:

> She genuflects; and our new priest
> Looks – only to falter in the Mass;

Even the altar boy has ceased
And his responses, now, alas,
Are not 'Amen' – but towards the door
He seems to sigh: *a stoir, a stoir.*

The book was the first in a series to be published jointly by
Messrs. Macmillan in London and Browne and Nolan in Dublin.
The directors of the local firm, which published education books,
withdrew in alarm and the literary venture came to an end.

The offending lyric was, surely, mild in tone. Actually, it was a
close rendering of a Spanish folksong, which had been translated
by Eithne MacCarthy, grand-daughter of Denis Florence
MacCarthy, poet-translator of plays by Calderon.

Soon after the Second Ecumenical Council came to an
inconclusive end, the Catholic Archbishop of Dublin consoled his
bewildered flock in a special message: 'You may have been worried
by much talk of changes to come. Allow me to reassure you no
change will worry the tranquility of your Christian lives.'

But the spirit of toleration is already spreading. Catholic doctors,
laymen and women, discuss now in the correspondence columns of
the *Irish Times* such subjects as contraception, divorce, the *Ne
Temere* decree, and courageously allow their names and addresses
to be printed. Ignorance still watches from its smoky cell.

Eight

THE PLAYWRIGHTS of the Abbey Theatre have a copious idiomatic speech of city and country upon which they can draw. But the ease with which they have been able to cram their note books with dialect and humorous sayings has not been without danger. They have advanced very little since the comicalities of rustic and slum speech were rediscovered. They are still, like Lover and Lever, fascinated by the externalities of overheard give-and-take. This vivacious dialect, which in real life is used as often as not to conceal rather than to reveal thought, interposes itself between them and the characters which they wish to analyse. As a result, their characterization is too often a form of patronage. Fortunately, our poets have avoided such temptation and their imaginative language is their own. There is not a word of direct dialect in *The Drover* by Padraic Colum or in *The Old Age Pensioner* by Joseph Campbell. Yet such is the subtle use of simple words in those lyrics that they are as new to us as the Irish countryside itself.

In his poems of city life, Seumas O'Sullivan had to find his own models and in a similar way, he succeeded without the ready aid of the vernacular speech used by James Joyce and Sean O'Casey. *The Piper* expresses the tragedy of slum life in simple words that are hard to forget. The old woman munching scraps on the doorstep of a Georgian house, the lamplighter stealing down back-streets into the past, the man watching the funerals go by on their way to Glasnevin – all these are not only precise in detail but have that subjective validity which counts most in art. How well the drabness of our older streets is expressed in this poem:

> There is hardly a mouthful of air
> In the room where the breakfast is set,
> For the blind is still down tho' it's late,

65

And the curtains are redolent yet
Of tobacco smoke, stale from last night.
There's the little bronze teapot, and there
The rashers and eggs on the plate,
And the sleepy canary, a hen,
Starts faintly her chirruping tweet . . .

In *The Miracle*, Seumas O'Sullivan mingled his meditative rhythm with those excitable little 'runs' which quicken our speech. The skill with which he could combine and transform these natural rhythms in lyrical measures is shown in this Edwardian period piece:

The sunlight shone down on the long road, deserted and
    silent;
No motor, nor cyclist, nor horseman, nor even –
To trouble its peace – a pedestrian,
Save only for me, who went silent,
And a young girl who passed me, demure,
And as fresh as the Spring, and as lovely,
And daintily stepping.
And yet as she passed me, I swear to you somebody
    coughed.
No merely civilian, inadequate, meaningless cough,
But a soldier's cough, chesty, profound,
And female-attention-compelling.
Yet the road was quite empty
Save only for me, who went silent,
And the lovely demure-stepping maid,
And the statue of Gough on his horse,
With his field marshal's baton.

Seumas O'Sullivan learned much of his art from the French lyric, from Samain, de Régnier and others. That is why his best-known lyrics are, as Ernest Boyd has said, deeply national enough to take on the air of cosmopolitanism in the best sense of the word. This quality will be found also in his prose. The short stories and impressions in *Mud and Purple* and in *Common Adventures* continue the mood of his verse. *In a Music Hall* brings back nights

66

by the Liffey side:

> Last of all, stepping swiftly, yet with a due sense of his all-importance, comes the little conductor, immaculately dressed. With a low bow, fall of grace, to the audience, he takes his place upon his chair.
>
> His right hand holds delicately the little ivory baton for a moment suspended in the air. The music begins and with the first note of it, his left hand comes to life.

The haze of tobacco smoke dims the Tivoli:

> Tune follows tune. Strong men and fluffily skirted girl dancers, conjurers with eloquent shirt cuffs, and comedians with their dreadful jokes, all move unceasingly like the figures of some uneasy dream. . . . But through all the deepening mist of vaguely moving figures and vaguer music, floats undimmed that delicate left-hand of the conductor – *a lily in hell.*

Forgotten types reappear in these essays, as in *Winter Sunlight* :

> It was all about me, but almost unnoticed until I arrived at the corner of Merrion Square. Then that undersized youth who bears his life miraculously amidst the chaotic traffic with such easy responsibility and incidentally changes the points on the tram lines, threw his small steel pointer in the air and caught it again with a fine precision.

The Winter sunlight shines on the flower girls sitting with their baskets, the book-sellers' window, the cripple with his crutch. Then clouds darken the streets and all seems to have been a dream. But as the poet arrives at the corner of Ely Place, the sunlight reasserts itself:

> It was shining now on the tall poplar trees amongst which George Moore walks in his garden and invented the story of his life.

67

Seumas O'Sullivan was as elusive as his own essays and poems of the side streets, courts and alleys of Georgian Dublin. For several months, as I have said, F. R. Higgins and I hovered around his small chemist shop near the Rathmines Town Hall. Sometimes we ventured in and bought a box of Beecham's Pills or a tin of Zambuk in the hope of getting a glimpse of the poet in his dispensary at the back of the shop. But our efforts were in vain, for he was too well hidden and we never saw even his shadow moving behind the rows of medicine bottles.

In much trepidation, I sent a lyrical passage from my first long narrative poem to Seumas O'Sullivan, begging his opinion of it. Months passed and then it came back to me with a brief note in shaky hand script from the poet, saying he was unable to give me any opinion of it. I was very disappointed and yet consoled by the fact that he had kept it beside him while mixing carminatives and flavouring jallop, for the two pages of the manuscript were stained with a number of interesting brown rings. Later he told me how, in his boyhood, the fashionable Victorian doctors of Rathmines, in morning dress and tall hat, drove in their open carriages to his father's shop and ordered powerful purgatives to be sent to Mrs. X, Mrs. Y, and other wealthy clients. They called these doses by the opprobious name of 'breech charges' and in that way revenged themselves on the respectability of the era.

I met Seumas O'Sullivan for the first time on a Saturday morning at the book barrows in Aston Lane just off the Quay soon after my first book had been published. In some confusion he apologized for being unable to give me an opinion of the fragment which I had sent him. Soon I was to realize that he was too sensitive and diffident to venture an opinion on new work although he edited the *Dublin Magazine* for more than twenty years and helped many young writers by publishing their first poems, short stories and essays. He consulted us frequently when in doubt over a contribution. He was tall, dark, handsome as a funeral horse, as one admirer expressed it, with an aloof eighteenth-century air. He carried a fine walking stick and at one time affected an ornate silver snuff box, the contents flavoured with tonquin bean. Whenever I took a pinch and gave way to a fit of sneezing, he looked at me in severe disapproval.

For a number of years I used to meet Seumas O'Sullivan every Friday morning at his home in Morehampton Road an hour or so after his ample breakfast, which consisted of orange, porridge, bacon and eggs, a chop, toast and marmalade. We sat in his sunny library with bookcases filled with rare volumes which he had collected or found for a few pence on the book barrows. Included among his treasures were books signed by William Blake, Samuel Taylor Coleridge and other writers. Usually, we spent some time discussing the lesser known eighteenth-century writers, about whom he knew so much. Then we sauntered citywards, stopping for a first drink at a tavern near Baggot Street Bridge. We strolled through St. Stephen's Green, along the Beaux Walk, and stopped again at O'Neill's public house in Anne Street. So by leisurely degrees we reached the Bodega in Dame Street and sat downstairs behind the great vats there at one of the small tables safe from intruders. Seumas O'Sullivan's manner was courteous but he had a surprisingly swift technique in getting rid of the occasional bore or drunk who is always such a problem in public houses.

I left him and went home to lunch during the Holy Hour, that period until three o'clock when all public houses were shut and wise drinkers adjourned to the Workman's Club on the Quay near Capel Street Bridge.

We met again about 4 o'clock and, dallying on our way at several hostelries – for the poet had his strict round of calls – we arrived at the Palace in Fleet Street, where R. M. Smyllie, Editor of the *Irish Times* held his daily session, surrounded by poets, novelists and journalists. Press correspondents, visitors to Dublin, found their way there but no employee or plain drinker from the Corporation depot on the opposite side of the road ventured beyond the glass-door of the inner saloon bar.

Before Seumas O'Sullivan and his wife, the well-known artist Estelle Solomons, settled in Morehampton Road, they lived in a Georgian mansion beyond Rathfarnham which had been owned by Buck Whaley, one of the eighteenth-century rakes. Every Saturday afternoon on my way to his house I passed the monstrous conglomeration of buildings owned by the Loreto nuns – Celtic Romanesque and Gothic overshadowing a graceful Georgian house. In the extensive demesne on the opposite side of the road which the nuns had acquired was another eighteenth-century house and through the trees I could see many plaster holy statues, all standing robed, in the open air. In the extensive fields beyond the convent which the nuns had bought was the house once owned by the Protestant patriot, orator, poet and wit, John Philpott Curran, and, hidden there in the wild among nettles was the grave of his daughter, Sarah, who had been the sweetheart of Robert Emmet. Despite public pleas, the nuns had allowed the roof of the house to fall in. Now only a heap of rubble marks the site.

The road led uphill and soon I passed the gate of St. Edna's the lay school which had been founded by Padraic Pearse. Turning the corner at the road top, I could see below the city and its spires and soon came to the gate lodge of the Grange, where Thomas Mac-Donagh had lived a few years before the Insurrection. Along the same road came A.E. every Saturday, walking slowly as he composed a new poem, but I never met him on the way.

Sometimes on those sunny afternoons I played rather unwillingly a polite game of croquet as awkwardly as Alice in Wonderland and always I was surprised at the dignity of the poet, an admirable host, who might have passed the week among his books instead of in the Bohemian taverns of Dublin. We spent the evening in the pleasant drawing-room with its wooden balcony and view of woods. Often I liked to stray into the walled orchard with its cabbage plots, rows of gooseberry, currant bushes, and at times, brush through the docken patch by the rivulet beyond the garden.

In those far off days, witty remarks spread among the festive poet's companions in Dublin and rapidly vanished into oblivion. Unfortunately, I can remember only a few of them for in the excited give-and-take of the taverns, where I drank small sherries, I was elated and the memory of jokes was insecure. On one occasion, Thomas Bodkin, the art critic, who had returned to Dublin on a brief visit, met an old friend at a literary gathering. He had grown an imperial and the purple-haired lady gazed at him admiringly.

'Tom,' she exclaimed, 'you look like an Old Master!'

'And you, my dear,' he replied ungallantly, with a bow, 'look like an old mistress.'

James Montgomery, the film censor, who was an intimate companion of Seumas O'Sullivan and Oliver Gogarty, was well known for his quick retorts, being perhaps the wittiest of those merrymakers. He summed up the difficulties of his office in an epigram, 'I'm between the Devil and the Holy See'. Montgomery had seen a London production of Henri Gheon's play, *St. Francis of Assisi*, in which the leading part was played by a notorious invert.

'What did you think of the performance?' he was asked by a friend.

'It was the Francis of a sissy,' he replied.

In his humorous, devious way, Seumas O'Sullivan was accustomed to attribute many of his own witty remarks and parodies to Gogarty, so it is difficult to decide which of them wrote the parody of that famous last line in a sonnet by Keats:

Silent, upon a peak in Darien.

The parody observes carefully the effective caesura of the original line:

Potent, behind a cart with Mary Ann.

A variation on an equally well-known sonnet by Wordsworth has a baroque effect:

Boss Sinclair rising naked from the sea,
Followed by Cox with seaweed-wreathed horn.

Sinclair was the owner of an antique shop and his friend Cox was a barrister who collected first editions. In one of his essays Seumas O'Sullivan has described mockingly Cox's collection, which was completely worthless. By changing a single word in A.E.'s lyric, 'I begin through the grass to be reconciled to the Lord', Seumas O'Sullivan completely changed its moral and gave it a touch of Persian mysticism. 'I begin through the glass to be reconciled to the Lord'. Of the old ladies who played bridge incessantly at the Arts' Club, the poet remarked, parodying a line of Marlowe:

Infinite bitches in a little room.

Borrowing from Wilde, he said of the Gaelic short-story writer, Padraic O'Conaire: 'He is drinking beyond our means.'

One evening, looking from the drawing-room window of his

house in Morehampton Road, he saw a man pushing a hand-cart with a small load of manure. 'I see that Paddy Kavanagh is moving. There go his furniture and effects'. Patrick Kavanagh, the well-known poet, had been a small farmer.

One day Seumas O'Sullivan met the cook of the Bailey Restaurant in a passage-way dressed in his white overall and high hat.

'I am His Holiness. You must kiss my big toe,' said the cook jokingly.

'I won't,' said the poet in pretended Protestant indignation, 'but I have often bowed to your joints.'

An Anglo-Irish Colonel remarked to him, 'I advertised the other day for a gardener and have just got a reply from a man who says he's a Protestant. I daresay it is all for the best'. 'Yes, in these days it is important to get a gardener who digs with the right foot.' This Irish expression means that the person in question is a Catholic or Protestant as the case may be.

When the Catholic Archbishop of Dublin decided that sinners who were infected with syphilis should be treated in our religious hospitals, there was much discussion in the newspapers.

'The *Irish Times* is all V.D.' said the poet, 'the *Irish Independent* is all D.V. (*Deus volens*).'

Fitzgerald Kenny, a well-known landowner and barrister in County Mayo, was Minister for Justice in the Free State Government. He was a good classical scholar but also a bitter-tongued Catholic.

'I'd like to see you burned,' he exclaimed during a half-serious argument with Seumas O'Sullivan. 'A case of little Latin and more grease.' The poet's knowledge of Latin was mostly pharmaceutical.

'What is fornication?' asked a pretty girl at a literary gathering. There was an embarrassed silence until he explained with a smile, 'Fornication, my dear, is the thief of time'.

On a Spring afternoon in County Wicklow, a young Englishman was much delighted at the playful lambs in the fields. Seumas O'Sullivan stooped and searching the grass, plucked a sprig of wild mint.

'You see,' he observed, 'God provides for everything.'

In the early days of the dramatic movement he played the part of the blind beggar in Yeats' play, *The King's Threshold.* As he groped across the stage, stick in hand, Oliver Gogarty, who was in one of the front seats, exclaimed joyously: 'There goes the Bard – blind again.'

The carpenter of the Gaiety Theatre, who was friendly with the literary groups, complained of some disparaging remarks about his craft. 'After all, Christ was a carpenter.

'But what about the scab who made the Cross?' said Seumas.

On the top of the Rathfarnham tram one evening, a young intoxicated painter swayed and spewed on the poet's shoulder.

'I have known W. B. Yeats for twenty years', the poet complained, 'and he never did that to me.' The remark was a far-reaching one for Yeats regarded the younger generation with disfavour after A.E. had gathered their early poems in a small anthology.

Nine

I

CAREFULLY HE BENT DOWN to light his pipe and I watched the tiny ritual flame of the match. Its brevity in the darkness brought me a pleasant hint of the wood-fire which would soon be ours. When the glow was gone, I became aware of a secret change as we walked along the country road. Something living, shy as rabbit or other creature of the night, was following us. Glancing sideways a few times, I saw what seemed the very shadow of a shadow moving with us. I noticed a great star in the sky. I must have been mistaken. How could a planet cast a shadow? I said nothing to my companion.

Many years later I found that I had not been mistaken. In a note to his book, *Poems from Selborne*, my friend, Anthony Rye wrote: 'The planets in full brightness are said by scientists to shadow. Gilbert White in his Journal and elsewhere mentions several times this phenomenon. which seems to have had a special fascination for him. 'Venus Shadows', 'Venus sheds her silvery light on the walls of my chamber' . . .

The road rang with winter beneath our feet, but the hedges, heavy with moisture, might have been laden with ripe berries and, at times, between them, the soft air from the midlands brought me a hint of sap at the turn of Spring, so that I fancied I could hear the birds stir in their sleep. On such a night, all the seasons, except Summer, seem to meet. Along many miles, the stars were coming out and I thought of their soft light in the bogland waters below the Hill of Allen.

'We must be near the mountains now,' I said, for the air had changed and seemed to flow from cold springs in the uplands. The storyteller plodded on without a word, his peaked hat pulled down, as though he had left a small hammer and last in the wood which we had just gone by.

We had spent the night before in a shebeen near the Pro-Cathedral and, punctual at six o'clock in the morning, we were

74

drinking porter in a public house, near the City Market, open for carters and stall-holders. Suddenly, Padraic O'Conaire remembered that he had a cottage in the country. As he had been downing quarts, I did not believe him, but fell in with his wish to leave the city. So we made our way to Kingsbridge and took a train to Naas. There I waited in the main-street, while he went into the office of the *Leinster Leader* to correct the proofs of his weekly article in Irish. After that, we strolled along small roads, from inn to inn, until the canal bridges were ringed greyly by their own reflections at twilight.

We came to a village, and passing several lighted windows, Padraic O'Conaire stopped to knock at a door. The woman of the house welcomed him and brought us into the kitchen. 'And how is Mrs. O'Conaire?' she asked. 'She had a bad attack of 'flu and is staying with relatives in Scotland. But I'm glad to say that she's feeling much better!'

I knew that Padraic had a wife and two children somewhere in London, but this was a surprise to me and yet I could not help admiring his air of grave concern and relief. The kettle was on the hob, but we did not wait for a cup of tea.

We crossed the street to a grocery store and there a large man, with his elbows on the counter greeted us. 'And how is Mrs. O'Conaire?' he asked. 'She's had a bad attack of 'flu, and is staying with relatives in Scotland, but I am glad to say that she's feeling much better.' We bought rashers and sausages, a loaf, butter, Canadian cheese, onions, a couple of candles and a dozen bottles of stout. I counted out the money, and with several parcels under our oxters, we went into the night.

'We're passing the Croppies Graveyard there on the left'.

We went by lengthening bushes until we came to an old iron gate. 'Bad luck to that donkey!' exclaimed Padraic as a dark form shook the dripping leaves and bounded past us. He lit a candle in the cottage room and said in a rueful tone, 'The tinkers have been here again'.

The floor was littered with the brown, green, yellow, pamphlets and booklets published by the Gaelic League. A bundle of blankets and car rugs were heaped in a corner, abandoned, no doubt, when a step had sounded on the road outside.

We dragged in wood and thin branches from the shed outside and piled them on the hearth. Soon the flames were warming up and while they were bullying the shadows, we opened our parcels. I noticed something exciting in the corner near the bedding, so, while Padraic was busy at the fire, I went over quietly, candle in hand. I was staring at a pair of silk stockings and knew by them that his Scottish mistress had long shapely legs. I thought of Etaira the night before and as I drew down in fancy a garter from her naked thigh, I felt faint with longing once more. Then, I forgot her. The frying-pan was a-sizzle and the delicious aroma of American bacon, sliced from the flitch, was curling upwards towards the roof. Supper was ready.

Afterwards, we sat by the fire, drinking stout, talking until midnight. Padraic told me of his wanderings throughout the country with his ass and cart, although I had already known them from his delightful book of essays *An Craobh Geagach*.

'The ass,' he explained, 'is of an idle disposition and has little regard for the stick. But as it was originally a desert animal, it has an ancestral fear of trees. So, I cut down several branches of rowan and fixed them in a sort of canopy over the shafts, and you should have seen how that ass took to the roads, and galloped around every corner, trying to escape from the rustle of the leaves!'

So he had come, followed by children, to the townland in County Galway, where his uncle was parish priest. Every year he came there and his uncle hastily dipped into the collection plate in his pocket and in that way got rid of his unwelcome nephew. Later, I wrote a lyric about his travels with his ass and cart, fancying that he drove from the midland into our legendary darkness:

> How can I deny that enchantment
> When berries grew scarlet
> And for twenty-six counties she went by
> The halfway house at a canter,
> Though I thought, had she sighted a barrel
> Growing at a door, she would stop,
> And the blackbird I carried for pleasure,
> Sharpening his beak in lamp-sugar,
> Sang to those branches?
> Torchlight, in Tara
> Had armed the rampart at night
> And I heard the harp and crowds dancing

For a queen that had been married,
But the cold rain blew them away
As a story, and by the dark roads
Where no farmer has strayed from the market,
The berries, grown black in the moonlight,
Hurry us onward.

'You should invent the plots for your narrative poems,' he said
to me that night. I had not the gift and so went on borrowing them
from myth and traditional lore.

We stayed for a week in the cottage, wandering for most of the
day around the countryside or climbing the slopes of Slieve Breac,
until we saw the Central Plain and the wide sky. Padraic stopped at
every small farmhouse and always I heard the same dialogue at the
half-door.

'And how is Mrs. O'Conaire?'

'She's had a bad attack of 'flu and is staying with relatives in
Scotland. But I'm glad to say she's feeling much better'.

Sometimes we sat by the Liffey Falls of Golden Water, a
corruption of the Gaelic name, The Fork of Drowning. These falls,
like those under the battlemented bridge at Poulaphouca, are no
more since the Liffey dam was built for the new reservoir. Wherever
I looked, that week, I found images. The long pastures were
bordered by narrow woods. As we walked under the trees, I thought
of far places in the Spring:

O we will hurry
South where the squirrels run a mile through boughs
From isle to isle, and in the hazels
The sunlight dances with green heels.

and

When mountain rocks are red with bracken
The fox may run unseen.

On Sunday morning, when all were at Mass, we leaned over the
high bridge of Poulaphouca, staring down at the cascade and the
dark pool below. We went over at last to the parapet on the opposite

77

side. Two girls smoking cigarettes by the riverside, smiled up at us in a sleepy way. 'They're the Bad Girls of the district,' said Padraic severely, leading me quickly away from the bridge.

On the next Saturday, we returned to the city on the top of the steam train. We passed through Blessington with wide street, polled trees and monument erected by a grateful tenantry to its landlord. The tram rattled down the long incline of the Embankment and we watched the city below. But we were going so fast that I could not count the crosses, smaller than milestones, raised in memory of the unfortunate drunkards who, on their way home at night, lay on the track and were run over by the last tram. So we arrived, unwashed, unshorn, at the tram-stables in Terenure, once known as Roundtown.

With his battered hat, shabby clothes, old topcoat and stout ashplant, Padraic O'Conaire looked like an outcast, a lasting symbol of the writer in Ireland, and many avoided him whenever they could. Once he and I were walking down Grafton Street at the fashionable hour and saw James Stephens a short distance from us. 'A hamus! A hamus!' called O'Conaire, hurrying forward, waving his stick. Stephens had heard him for he quickened his pace. We tried to catch up with him, but when we turned the corner of Anne Street, he was gone. No doubt, he had sought refuge in one of the Art Shops.

Nevertheless, Padraic O'Conaire, like the Russian writers, had great respect for the short story. He shaped each of his by telling it casually to friends and strangers, as he roamed from bar to bar. Then, when he was ready to set it down in his neat handwriting, he washed, shaved, put on his secret Sunday suit and sat at his desk in a top room which was reserved for him in the headquarters of the Gaelic League at Parnell Square.

Some years ago, Sean J. White told me a remarkable story. Padraic O'Conaire called one night to the offices of *The Connacht Tribune* in Galway to collect ten shillings due to him for an essay. The Editor gave him the half-note and he handed it back to him in payment of a loan. They left the office and went down the road to a public house. On their way they met a Professor from the University College, a perfervid Gael. Padraic drew him aside and asked for the loan of ten bob to stand his friend a drink. The Professor, weary, no doubt, of being touched too often in the Irish language, said he had no change. When the sound of his footsteps faded away down the street, Padraic turned to the Editor and said in a grave tone which was unlike him: 'The day will come when that man will unveil a statue to me . That day came.

Ten

I

WHEN I CAME to the little town of Gort, the ancient royal stories of Guaire and Maravan vanished from my mind as night fell. I can only remember the empty market place that seemed to lie in wait for a fair, three melancholy foreigners who had come there to sell native frieze, and a girl who stared into nothingness with a brazen face.

The morning sun was still clouded when I saw for the first time the Woods of Coole. I found a small unlocked gate and in a few minutes I stood within a dark plantation that was lit only by the cold sharp silver of the hollies. I wondered if it were the nameless 'wicked wood' of the poem or shady Kyle-dortha. Hastening along a winding, foot-beaten track, I came into a thinner wood, and as I waited there, I grew aware that there was secret honey around me. This surely must be Pairc-na-carraig,

> Where the wild bees fling their sudden fragrances
> On the green air.

I had only known those deeper woods of the south, in which the very dews stir heavily from a footstep: but in these thin western woods every tiny sound of the leaves was delicate. In great delight I moved softly there and not without scruples, for I was trespassing in the solitude where the poet had found so much of his inspiration. The trees had become darker, wilder again, and, because I could see a sunnier wood beyond them, I stayed under those boughs. If I remained here long enough the unexpected might happen, for I was certain that I had come to that secret place:

> Dim Pairc-na-tarav, where enchanted eyes
> Have seen immortal, wild, proud shadows walk.

80

I closed my eyes but nothing happened. Then, as I opened them again, I thought I saw a rich blue gleam dart through the distant leaves. I could not be mistaken and so I strode forward cautiously. A moment later I saw the blue flash again. Perhaps it was only a peacock searching in the grasses, but why was it moving so rapidly? Coming nearer, I peeped through the leaves and saw, to my chagrin, that I had mistaken for bird or spirit a tall sportsman, wearing an unusual raincoat of sky-blue watered silk, and carrying the rods and fierce tackle of his craft. Believing that I had strayed into the wrong demesne and that I had been dreaming foolishly in ordinary woods, I was about to turn away, when I noticed that the angler was crossing a wide lawn towards the portico of a Georgian mansion. To my complete astonishment, I saw that it was the poet himself.

Bewildered by that unexpected encounter, I hurried through the underwoods and, in a few minutes, had lost my way. I came to long paths, grass-grown, hedged with wild pale privet. I wandered up and down in confusion for, though I was at the edge of the woods, I no longer wanted to count them. At last I escaped from those hedges, where wildness was only neglect, and found myself on grey ledges of rock that dwindled among a few rushes growing by a small lake. Across the water was another wood. This must be Shan- walla, but I saw with a pang that the wild swans had gone.

I sat down on a rock near the water's edge, but mocking thoughts midged me from every side. The week before, I had crossed Lough Gill and, with great persistence and guile, had asked the boatman the name of every island we passed. As we came to the far end of the lake, he pointed to a rocky islet with high tufts of heather, a few sloe bushes and a small patch of grass, and he had said: 'That's Innisfree'. I could hear his voice again and it had become horribly confidential.

'Would you believe it now, two ladies came here last year all the way from London to see that rock. They said it must be Innisfree, and that there was a poem written about it, though, round here, it is known as Rat Island. They brought their lunch with them, and stayed there for two solid hours, writing postcards to their friends.'

Crude-coloured postcards with fragments of scrawled exclamations danced before my sight and like those cards that Alice saw in Wonderland, they became suddenly shrill and in a pack they ran against me and the woods grew harsh with magpies, and stumbling

81

blindly through brambles, I hurried along to the grass-grown paths again. I came at length to some outbuildings. A man was standing with a bucket and brush outside a stable door. He told me that Mr. Yeats was staying in a house on the opposite side of the road and that in a week or two he was going to Ballylee. I had heard that the poet had acquired an old Norman keep there.

The sun hid suddenly, and a fairy wind blew me, hat in hand, across the road. But the eddy of dust was gone even while I hesitated before the knocker.

II

Somehow I found myself in a plain room, timidly picking at a fish and wondering if the poet had caught it himself. His own lunch was over and so he leaned from a sofa opposite the table, wearing a brown velvet shooting-jacket. A pallid mask of his features stared blindly from a glass case in the corner of the room.

'The imagination must be disciplined, when it is young. Therefore, study the Jacobean lyrics, Donne, the poems of Landor. . . .'

His voice rose and fell in a lulling monotone, while secretly, I cursed the fish. It might have come from the cauldron of the elder gods, might have held the very smell of knowledge, for, despite my desperate efforts, it would not grow smaller, and its tiny stickles seemed to threaten my very existence.

'Verse should be ascetic, the beauty of bare words. . . .'

While he was speaking I seized the opportunity of pushing away the bewitched plate very gently.

'Master,' I said to myself in youthful enthusiasm, for I felt in happier mood, 'must not poetry sow its wild oats?'

I could hear that inner voice, despite me, imitating his chanting tone. But aloud I asked some polite question, to which he replied: 'Poetry needs the symbolic, that which has been moulded by many minds. The Japanese, when they hold their sacred processions, are accustomed to disguise themselves in the grotesque masks and armour of their ancestors. . . .'

'I want,' he said later on, 'to see a neo-Catholic school of young poets in this country.' He spoke of Jammes, Péguy, and Claudel,

82

and said much that I could not follow at the time, for I had been cast into a mild trance by the gleam of the great signet ring, upon his waving hand. I could not help watching that tremendous ring for I thought at the time that it had been fashioned by an artist of the Renaissance. But even in that trance I was trying to defend myself from the religious novelty which he was evolving. How could we learn to write the traditional songs of repentance before we had known those 'merry sins' of which Synge had spoken. I thought of the extravagant Gaelic poetry of the eighteenth century. Once more the strapping heroine of 'The Midnight Court' was railing against aged bridegrooms, denouncing the celibacy of the clergy. She was proving to her own satisfaction that it was heretical for these tonsured young men to live in a state of single bliss. Once more the Mangaire Sugach was reeling from another parish with a satire on his tongue, and in a distant tavern, O'Tuomey was filling his till with the fine words of his fellow-craftsmen.

'I have to catch a train at 4 o'clock,' exlaimed the poet, hastily rising from the sofa.

The sun was shining again, here and there, among the seven woods when we came to the door. As I stood with downcast head upon the threshold he must have noticed my depression, despite his short sight, for suddenly he cried above me in majestic tones: 'You must come and see me again, when I am in my castle!'

Eleven

DURING MY EARLY TWENTIES I was tempted constantly by superstition and found it hard to resist its wiles. The discovery of our own mythology and epic stories by the poets of the Irish Literary Revival excited my imagination and I cycled with delight to many places associated with legend and enchantments – from the Glen of the Madmen in County Kerry to the Twelve Pins of Connemara and the Poisoned Glen in Donegal. The armies of Queen Maeve on the march, the defence of Ulster by Cuchullain – all these stories from the Tain obsessed me. In particular, I was attracted by the earliest of our sagas – the *Intoxication of the Ulstermen*, which tells how the Northern warriors, after a great banquet, drove – much the worse for drink – throughout the countryside and did not stop until they found themselves, to their bewilderment, in the enemy territory of the South and were locked in an oriental palace of iron, under which great fires were kindled. Equally fascinating were the tales of Fionn and his Fianna, hunting wild boar and deer through the great Munster Forest, pursuing them down wooded glens, along the slopes of the mountains or crossing to the Isle of Arran off Scotland. Moreover, there were the Songs and Lamentations of Oisin and his Colloquy with St. Patrick on his return, after three centuries, in Tir na nOg. These pagan figures of the heroic age became as real to me as the religious figures of my childhood, and the Celtic religion, of which vestiges had survived, despite the care and toil of monks, had the appeal of a lost cause. I had come aware also of that invisible Ireland into which one might at any moment step. A few minutes there could be counted as a year here and the centuries passed there as quickly. So we have the story of Oisin, who was brought by Niamh across the ocean to the Land of the Ever Young. Nera, another poet, who ventured beyond the watch-fires on the night of Samhain into the other land, stayed for a year there, married and returned. But he had only been a few seconds away, for Maeve and her companies were still at feast.

With a headful of stories, I cycled about County Dublin, past ruined castles or Peel towers or over the Military Road by the Barracks, erected there by the British after the Rebellion of 1798 and still known incorrectly as the Hell Fire Club.

When temptation took the form of women, my difficulties were increased. The first whom I met was Ella Young. Pale, ethereal, dressed in grey flowing silks, she was about fifty years of age and looked like an ancient priestess or vestal virgin. She lodged in a small red-brick house in a terrace just beyond Harold's Cross and, on the first occasion when I came to see her in the afternoon, she lit a joss stick. I felt a dim, irreligious delight as the little haze of incense floated towards the ceiling. She was a devoted follower of A.E. and her poems, like those of Susan Mitchell, were of his kind. But though she, too, was a theosophist, her interests were quite different. A.E. was a student of the Sacred Books of the East: Ella Young concentrated on the Irish Cycle of Gods and Legends. Her cold grey eyes became luminous and she was strangely remote as she spoke of the Tuatha De Danann, the divine race, and her days seem to have been spent in visions. In particular, she was a devotee of Mannanaun Mac Lir, but, being so serious herself, she never referred to his shape-changing and pranks as the God of Hilarity.

Often in the summer, when Ella Young was staying at Bahana in a small farmhouse in a hidden corner of Glencree, I cycled out to see her, sometimes by the Scalp and the woods of Enniskerry or over Killakee mountain and down the narrow Glencree road past the ancient oak wood, in which Synge used to wander. In the little parlour she spoke to me of the old beliefs and I found it difficult to resist the influence of her visionary ways and looks. She had come to lodge there because of an old story that in one of the upper glens of Djouce, the children of Diarmuid and Grainne, those lovers who had been pursued by the jealous Fionn, had been fostered. There, of an evening, she listened to the elemental music and told me how she used to hear across the boglands of Donegal the distant sound of silver trumpets. When I left her, I was aware of all those forgotten multitudes of the past, as I cycled through the twilight by loose stone walls, rowan trees, hillside heather.

In this way the temptation increased and, lying in the heather near

85

the source of the Liffey under the morning lark-song or climbing past boulders into the upper glens and gullies of the Connemara mountains, I was aware of our imaginative heritage.

II

One day I set out from the Lake Hotel at Glendalough, and crossing the narrow strip between the two lakes, went up between the trees past a waterfall near the ruins of a small ancient church. Below I could see, among the pine trees, the glitter of the lower lake and the waterfall above the western shore thinned by summer. After a short climb up the shady path, I came to the upper glen of Luggala and soon I was crossing over the last ridge. I looked down into the long, narrow Glenmalure, with its reedy flats and the river winding its way towards Grianaun and the open hilly country beyond.

I came down, a brook beside me, with many little falls, towards the river, and below in the glen I could see the figure of a tall woman, veiled and dressed in black, followed by a wolfhound. I remembered suddenly that Maud Gonne stayed sometimes at Glenmalure and I guessed that it must be she – no doubt, on a round of corporal acts of mercy. I stopped at the first cottage in the glen to enquire where Madame Gonne McBride was staying. A little old peasant woman came to the door and replied, much to my surprise, in French. I knew instantly that I had come to the right house. As I replied in halting school French, I heard inside the cottage an extraordinary medley of sounds as of a small menagerie and aviary: chattering of a monkey, wrangle of a parrot, pretty twitters of canaries. The old woman brought me into a kitchen, bright and gay, for the white-washed walls were decorated with patterns of foxglove, buttercup and other wild flowers, and I knew that Maud Gonne or her son-in-law had painted them.

In a short time, Maud Gonne returned and told me, as I had guessed, that she had been visiting the sick wife of a farmer who lived about a mile down the glen. I had met her first in her house in St. Stephen's Green and dined there in a large room which was furnished like a kitchen, with scrubbed dresser and table. The other guests were W. B. Yeats and Dermot O'Byrne, better known as the composer, Arnold Bax, who later became Master of the King's

86

Musick. I met Arnold Bax on the landing while he waited with a humility and awe which surprised me, despite my own reverence for the great poet. Unfortunately, I cannot remember anything which Yeats said on that memorable evening – perhaps I was too shy to collect my thoughts.

On that night in Glenmalure, after supper, Maud Gonne talked to me late into the night. Much to my surprise, she spoke of the heroic past, of the visions she had seen often and of her awareness of the Invisible Ireland. She, too, like Ella Young, seemed to change. She was aged and wrinkled but her eyes, with their golden circles, were unusual and reminded me of the astonishing beauty of her early years. I remembered the many poems which Yeats had written about her and realized for the first time how greatly they had influenced one another. She had drawn him for a time into revolutionary politics, but he had lured her into the invisible land of the Ever Young. There came into my mind that neglected poem of his, 'The Old Age of Queen Maeve', which tells how the children of Maeve dug into an enchanted hill to rescue the blue-eyed Caer:

> And all that night, and all through the next day
> To middle night, they dug into the hill.
> At middle night great cats with silver claws,
> Bodies of shadow and blind eyes like pearls,
> Came up out of the hole, and red-eared hounds
> With long white bodies came out of the air
> Suddenly, and ran at them and harried them.

The poet had turned from his narrative to tell of Maud Gonne:

> Friend of these many years, you too had stood
> With equal courage in that whirling rout;
> For you, although you've not her wandering heart,
> Have all that greatness, and not hers alone,
> For there is no high story about queens
> In any ancient book but tells of you;
> And when I've heard how they grew old and died,
> Or fell into unhappiness, I've said,
> 'She will grow old and die, and she has wept!'
> And when I'd write it out anew, the words,

> Half crazy with the thought, She too has wept!
> Outrun the measure.

That night, as I drifted into sleep, I could hear the noise of the torrent outside and I struggled in vain against the superstition of Ella Young and Maud Gonne, for I seemed to catch within the waters the tinkle and running of many sweet sounds and chords.

The next morning, as we sat at breakfast and I was tapping with my spoon on a speckled egg, Maud Gonne told me how she had been aware in the night of those invisible beings she had known in the past. Much to my embarrassment, she thanked me for she was certain that my youth and eagerness had brought them around the cottage. I remained silent, knowing how desperately I had struggled against superstition, being determined to use those stories as an imaginative form and experiment since, in the poverty of our history, due to centuries of conquest these were all that had been left to us. The day passed and, not wishing to spend another night so near to fairy music, I pleaded an excuse and, saying farewell to my hostess, I walked the three miles as fast as I could to the safety of the small hotel near the cataract at the end of Glenmalure.

Twelve

I

'COME IN, COME IN' – Joseph Campbell would exclaim as he stood on the doorstep of his house. Every time I visited him, I fancied that I heard his cheerful Northern voice echoing from Kilmolin to Glencree. Often at the weekend other writers walked up the long steep road, breath after breath, from Enniskerry to Kilmolin. There was a pleasant sitting-room, low-ceilinged, with a turf-fire: the shelves lined with the gold-green volumes of the Irish Text Society and slim books of Maunsel & Co. with ivory, olive, brown bindings. Above the shelves were drawings of Donegal mountains and tarns, abrupt contrasts of black and white, which the poet had made in order to pay the expenses of a walking tour in the Glenties.

Sometimes in the twilight, Joseph Campbell and I went up the high bracken field to the last ridge behind the house. As we sat beneath the loose stone wall of the larch wood, we could see below all that region which he describes in the Foreword to *Earth of Cualann*:

> Wild and unspoilt, a country of cairn-crowned hills and dark, watered valleys, it bears even to this day something of the freshness of the heroic dawn. Wandering in any field of it, one can still hear Fionn's command to Oisin: 'Hold the chase of Laighen of sword-blades, of Osraighe and of Sliabh Cualann'.

I was aware of the images through which he evoked the past.

> The burning inn at the crossways,
> The Fian tracking the boar,
> The queen riding northward
> With her horseboys and women.

89

Joseph Campbell had spent several years in London, where he became Secretary of the Irish National Literary Society soon after the young Donegal poet, Thomas Boyd, had disappeared with the funds. He became, also, a member of the Imagist Group. He returned to Ireland with his wife, Nancy, who was also a poet, and settled down on the borderland of Wicklow. His early lyrics drew much from folklore, but in his middle forties, when I met him, he had come to believe in austerity of line and image. So he looked sternly on the youthful bluebelling, lushing and thrushing of my first book. He reviewed it in *New Ireland* with a severity that surprised me, listing a number of inaccuracies in my descriptions of Nature, such as:

By bluebells glimmering through russet ferns. . . .

Did I not know that bluebells came out in spring? I was puzzled for I had certainly seen the blue and brown together. In the controversy which began in the periodical, a letter-writer pointed out that the deciduous ferns remained long into the winter.

Had not Fionn pledged, 'Loudly to loose the ferrets of a thousand spears'? Campbell pointed out that the ferret is set silently. A correspondent replied correctly that the adjective 'loudly' referred to the verb 'pledged'. Another suggested that I used a similar word, 'ferret' which means the silk sling used in casting a spear. Indefensible, however, was the phrase, 'the wren's flutter and warble', because that tiny bird is as nimble, as quiet, as a mouse. Other correctors were more considerate. Dr. Douglas Hyde reminded me that the accent in 'Fianna' is on the first syllable not on the second. Dr. Sigerson remarked with a smile that I had only provided one meal of broiled trout from Loch Leane for the lovers, Diarmuid and Grainne, during their wanderings through the forests and glens.

This poetic castigation was a useful lesson and I could not complain because the controversy which went on for five weeks sent the book into a second impression.

Some months after the Rising, a few of us sat under the Raven's Rock on the northern slope of Glencree, listening as Joseph Campbell read out to us in vibrant tones his new poem, 'Raven's Rock', a parade of Irish heroes from the remote past to Easter Week

90

1916, which begins:

> The line of the hills is a song.
> Abhna, Aa-na-craebhi,
> Places of trees and rivers,
> Praise God with their sweetness.
> The lake shines, darker than a hound's eye.

While he recited, we could see the distant gleam of Lower Lough Bray, through a gap, below the shadowy cliffs, the two firs and the white-washed cottage where Synge stayed when he was writing *In the Shadow of the Glen*. Below us was the ancient oakwood in which he had brooded so often.

II

Early on a sunny morning, Joseph Campbell and I, ashplant in hand, set out on the thirty-mile walk to the Seven Churches at Glendalough. We climbed the long winding road past Lough Bray and the small upper lake, to the bare plateau, lingering for a few minutes under the lark-song at the little bridge over the bog-brown rivulet which so soon becomes the Liffey. At Sally Gap, we reached heatherlands where there is not a habitation for fifteen miles except a game-keeper's lodge. We went down into the shadowy defile of Glenmacanas, by the steep cataract, and came at dusk to a mild valley, pleasant with streams and clusters of hazel. In twenty minutes we had reached the cross-roads at Laragh, a mile from Glendalough.

We stayed for some days at the old-fashioned hotel between the two lakes. It was owned by an elderly man with three middle-aged daughters, large, big-hipped, formidable in aspect. Campbell named the two elder sisters, Goneril and Regan. The youngest, who had yellow hair and red cheeks, like a huge doll, became our Cordelia. When one of the three served us at table, we shook with secret mirth and had to invent amusing stories to avert suspicion. Daily, Goneril, Regan and Cordelia laboured in the kitchen, boiling, roasting chickens and basting ducks, preparing ample puddings and pies for lunch and dinner. Eventually, the three big sisters succumbed to the heat and toil.

Each day, we went along the lake road beyond the fir-trees, to the ruined buildings, flooded by mountain gullies, where, in the last century, hundreds of men worked in the lead mines. At the weekend, the miners, money in pocket, drove on jaunting car to the City, where they boozed in public house, and set out at midnight on the long return journey, bawling ditties as they crossed Calrai bog. A crone lived in a hovel near the ruins, long after the lead mine was closed down, refusing the last consolations of religion, because, like that royal hetaera, the Old Woman of Beara, she remembered the strong men she had clasped when she was young and as vigorous as they were. Several times, as we talked of her, Campbell told me with great amusement of an uncle of his, a priest who had wearied of Church restrictions. He set up a bordel in a town in Normandy and prospered there.

A few years later, Joseph Campbell, F. R. Higgins and I were at Glendalough. About one o'clock in the morning, we walked along the road by the moonlit lake. Having had several pints of Guinness, Higgins and I were feeling so burly that we could not refrain from singing at the top of our voices a well-known seashanty:

> I took her to a tavern and I treated her to wine,
> Little did I think she belonged to the rakish kind,
> I handled her, I dandled her, and found to my surprise,
> She was nothing but a fire-ship rigged up in a disguise.

Guinness bellowed the chorus:

> She'd a dark and a rolling eye,
> And her hair hung down in ringalets,
> She was a nice girl a decent girl
> But one of the rakish kind.

Memory of the rollicking past, when the lead mines were open and silver was sometimes got, hurried our voices on. Suddenly Campbell stopped and said: 'This is a holy place'.

In the silence, after he left us, we were abashed. We, too, respected those centuries when we had a small, independent Church of our own.

We could see on the far shore of the lake and eastward, clear in the moonlight, the Celtic-Romanesque churches, the oratories beside the tombs, and the peaked cap of the Round Tower.

III

During the British recruiting campaign in Ireland, when the First Great War was becoming more frightful, G. K. Chesterton spoke to a fashionable, matinee audience in the Theatre Royal, calling for many more thousands of volunteers to fight for Catholic Belgium and other small nations except our own. The Chairman, an elderly Judge, whose name I have forgotten, thanked the poet, assuring him that all but a tiny minority were loyal to the Throne.

'That is a lie!'

The accusing voice rang from the Gallery and its echoes seemed to me to resound among the Dublin hills. The protest was made by another poet – Joseph Campbell. Sitting beside him, I trembled with nervousness, as his body shook in rage. The Judge, alarmed and evidently thinking that gunmen were gathering in the stalls and scene-dock, hastily closed the meeting, while G. K. Chesterton sat on the stage in complete bewilderment.

IV

Joseph Campbell was elected to the first *Sinn Féin* Council of County Wicklow and was so shocked by its jobbery that he denounced the members for their nepotism and graft. His speech was widely reported in the press, causing much resentment in his neighbourhood. So, when the Civil War started, he was arrested as a Republican sympathizer, imprisoned in Mountjoy, without trial, and later, kept with hundreds of others behind barbed wire in the internment camp on the Curragh. He wrote a Jail Journal, which has not been published, and several poems. Here is one.

It was a time of trouble – executions,
Dearth, searches, nightly firing, balked escapes –
And I sat silent, while my cellmate figured

Ruy Lopez' Gambit from the 'Praxis'. Silence
Best fitted our mood: we seldom spoke.
'I have a thought,' he said, tilting his stool.
'We prisoners are so many pieces taken,
Swept from the chessboard, only used again
When a new game is started'. 'There's that hope,'
I said, 'the hope of being used again.
Some day of strength, when ploughs are out in March,
The Dogs of Fionn will slip their iron chains
And, heedless of torn wounds and failing wind,
Will run the old grey Wolf to death at last.'
He smiled, 'I like your image. My fat Kings,
And painted Queens, and purple-cassocked Bishops
Are tame, indeed, beside your angry Dogs!'

Disillusioned by such injustice, the poet emigrated to the United States, after his release two years later. He set up an Irish School of Studies in New York, and, when it failed, became a Lecturer at Fordham University. Having spent twelve years in exile, he returned to Ireland only to find, like Oisin after the Fianna, that the heroic age was gone.

Thirteen

I

SOME TIME AGO, I found a bit of paper on which I had jotted down a few notes about my first visit to James Joyce in Paris during the early 'Twenties. I had strayed along the *Rue de l'Annonciation, the Rue de la Conception,* the *Rue de l'Assumption* and other holy streets before I found the flat in which he was living with his small family. Critics have assured us that Mrs. Joyce was a handsome woman. In fact, she was homely and plain. Her son and daughter were as plain, and the latter, poor child, had a squint. To my surprise, all spoke among themselves the Italian of Trieste.

We had roast chicken and salad for supper. Afterwards, Joyce began to question me about literary affairs in Dublin. It was obvious, despite his air of aloofness, that he was curious about all that was happening there. 'Yeats, is he still living in Merrion Square?' 'Yes, he has a large wooden lectern in his drawing-room with a mystic Arabic book on it. They say that it is upside down! Guests can only come to his Monday evenings by invitation and Lennox Robinson is the Chucker-Out. However, on one occasion Yeats saw a young man there who had not been invited. He stalked up to him and said arrogantly, "I do not know you. Please leave my house." The poor fellow who had been educated at Oxford and wrote excellent reviews for the *Irish Statesman,* slunk out.'

'And does A.E. still cycle in from Rathgar to Plunkett House?'

'Yes, but they say that despite the exercise, he is putting on weight.'

'Has Seumas O'Sullivan given up the pharmacy in Rathmines near the Town Hall?'

'No, he's still there. We meet every week in the Palace.'

Finally he asked me, 'Does Gogarty still live in Ely Place?'

Some weeks later, as we were sitting in a cheap café in a side-street under the shadow of Saint Sulpice, drinking Pernod Fils,

95

Joyce, after a long silence, mentioned Yeats again. His remark was so surprising that I keep it in Italian: 'La poesia de Mangan e de Yeats è quella di segatora di chi sela fa da solo.'

Seeing that I was puzzled, he explained that Mangan and Yeats in their love-poems, both wrote in a reverential, remote way. He emphasized their obsession with hands, quoting Mangan and pointing to the frequency with which Yeats refers to pearl-pale hands. I realised that he was only acquainted with the early twilight poems. As I glanced at the drooping figure, I wondered if he had been addicted in youth to our national sin.

II

When Joyce was leaving Dublin, he borrowed as much money as he could from Oliver Gogarty, Seumas O'Sullivan and other friends who could ill-afford to help him. Indeed, he touched Seumas O'Sullivan for tooth-brush, carbolic powder, sponge and other small goods from his father's shop. In his memory, or in secret notebooks, he had stored their puns, jokes, indecent parodies, verses and Limericks.

None of us dared to mention the name of Joyce to Oliver Gogarty, who resented rightly, despite its comicality, the caricature of him in *Ulysses*. Frequently, on a Thursday afternoon at five o'clock, I called to see him in his surgery at Ely Place. Handsome, with flashing, rimless glasses, he had not lost his rakish look, though for many years he was a teetotaler owing to a tendency towards hardening of the arteries. One evening, he felt my wrist and I was alarmed when he informed me in his flippant half-serious way, that I had the same tendency.

He repeated to me, whenever I called, his latest witticisms. Most of these were pedantic, had been composed at night and involved a knowledge of classical tags: so I had to pretend that I understood them and shared his mirth. When he recited one of his poems, he hammered out the measure on the nearest side-table or on the back of a mahogany chair. At the time, I thought them frigid and academic. Some years later, when he had begun to drink ale again, he confessed to me, after he had rapped out the metre of a poem on the counter of a bar, that he had been inspired by Macaulay's *Lays of Ancient Rome.*

One evening he asked me to call for him at Jervis Street Hospital. As he was putting on his overcoat and scarf, he declaimed a long Rabelaisian passage in which he described the epic begetting of Gargantua. I listened in dread, lest the nuns and nurses passing by would overhear the rollicking lines about that gigantic copulation, which have never appeared in a book.

Later, when he had become a friend of Yeats in the Senate, Gogarty told me of his discovery that Cleopatra had twins by Anthony who were named the Sun and Moon. 'How Yeats would love to use that!' he exclaimed gleefully.

Gogarty's own poem *Leda and the Swan* undoubtedly influenced Yeats, though it is possible that the poet drew on his early memory of a copy of a painting by Michelangelo discreetly placed over a lofty doorway in the National Gallery at Trafalgar Square. No doubt, he took a hint from the last stanza of his friend's poem:

> When the hyacinthine
> Eggs were in the basket –
> Blue as at the whiteness
> Where a cloud begins;
> Who would dream there lay there
> All that Trojan brightness;
> Agamemnon murdered:
> And the Mighty Twins?

Oliver Gogarty had so frank, so happy-go-lucky an air, that it was impossible to affront him. When the Irish Academy of Letters offered an award of fifty pounds for the best volume of verse published in 1936, my *Collected Poems* had just appeared. The rival volume was by Lord Moyne. Yeats, who could not resist a title, found out that, at the closing date for the competition, I was a month over the age of forty and argued that this disqualified me. Stephen Gwynn thought that such disqualification would be unworthy of the Academy and Yeats hastily withdrew his opposition. When I asked Gogarty if he had spoken in my favour, he replied: 'Good Heavens, I wouldn't dream of opposing Yeats'.

He said it with so joyful a smile that I found it impossible to be annoyed with him.

'Let's go down to the Kipps,' exclaimed Oliver Gogarty, as he was driving me home from a party in his sports car at one o'clock in the morning. He was a reckless driver and we sped along the empty streets, over Butt Bridge, turned by Amiens Street Railway Station, passed Frenchman's Row and came to Mabbot Street. We saw the ruined houses, windows boarded up, dirty laneways in dim moonlight. He stopped outside a deserted house of ill-fame, the engine running softly in its oils. Leaning back, he recalled merry times in Night-town – as it was named by Joyce, who had evoked it in gloomy tones of thrilled horror. While he talked, I was aware of the Victorian Dream of Bad Women: Oblong Mary, whose name may have been Le Blanc, Piano Kate, Fresh Nelly, Liverpool Kate, Mrs. Mack, Mrs. Lepel – and the incomparable Mrs. Becky Cooper, keeper of the main shebeen. He recited to me his ballad of Ringsend.

> I will live in Ringsend
> With a red-headed whore,
> And the fan-light gone in
> Where it meets the hall-door;
> And listen each night
> For her querulous shout,
> As at last she steals in
> And the pubs empty out.

I had known the last of Night-town when it was difficult for a seedy man to walk down Grafton Street after dark without being accosted by pretty, well-dessed relievers from its purlieus, lurking in the shadowy doorways of the closed fashion shops.

'Goodnight Duckie, anything doing?' 'What's on your mind, luv?'

It was pleasant in winter to sit in one of the kitchens, a glowing fire in the closed range, drinking G.P. Every customer had to stand a round to the girls and the bawd. Usually, it cost ten shillings – a large sum at that time. Guinness – the drink of dock-labourers and whores – gave strength to husbands who found there what they lacked upstairs at home. As they looked at the row of willing girls, they felt, no doubt, like satraps choosing among concubines and after they had gulped down a few more glasses of stout, stumbled up the ricketty stairs with their purchase.

I told Gogarty how I had been in a shebeen one night with Padraic O'Conaire, the Gaelic writer, who was known in the Kipps as Paddy Conary. Suddenly a pretty girl who had consumed, no doubt, too many half-pints, leaped into the middle of the floor and began to dance wildly. Faster, faster, she whirled around, her skirts flying higher and higher. Before we could avert our eyes in modesty, we saw the illegal tricolour of the Irish Republic of her petticoat, slip and knickers, were a flag of green, white, and gold. This was audacious lingerie, because the lorries of the Black and Tans rattled through the streets after curfew and at any moment armed men might rap with the butts of their colt revolvers on the door. Padraic O'Conaire, whom I much admired, borrowed a pound from me and I was surprised to learn some weeks later from one of the girls that he had spent the night with her.

I became friendly with a jolly girl who lived on a small farm in County Wicklow with her father. Often, when she was in a sportive mood, she came down to the Kipps and abandoned herself for a few nights to the Devil. The husbands and young men who coupled with her had to strive hard for most of the night – between snatches of drowsing – so vigorously did she make them yield up to her the strength which they had gained from Guinness.

Once she told me of a girl who, much to her horror, found herself in bed with a priest. As she spoke, I seemed to see him hurrying through the chilly streets in the early morning, furtively saluting the few who passed him, confessing hastily to another priest before he said Mass.

Both of us had been silent for a while. Then, Oliver Gogarty glanced at his wrist-watch, and started the engine. We drove from the shadows of the past, by ruined houses, windows boarded up, dirty lanes in dim moonlight, then sped along the lighted thoroughfare, passing recklessly the Four Angels, one of them with a sword, near O'Connell Bridge.

IV

Oliver Gogarty was a successful, professional man, an eminent throat specialist, who lived sedately, liked high society, was charming in a drawing-room and kept his diverting, improper parodies for his occasional visits to a tavern. Even if he had never published anything nor emerged as a fine poet in his own right, he would have been remembered as a brilliant, witty talker, an arch-mocker whose exuberance and persistent gaiety were a continual surprise.

During the Civil War, Gogarty was caught, almost despite himself, in the swirl of violent politics and made bitter enemies when he took the side of his old friend, Arthur Griffith, the founder of Sinn Féin. His hatred of De Valera was obsessional: for he saw in him a chilly blend of Machiavellianism and Puritanism. On one occasion, after De Valera had gained power, he stopped in the middle of a broadcast from Radio Éireann, his voice trembling with rage, as he denounced the arch rebel. Immediately, he was cut off by the engineers. I happened, by chance, to be listening and was deeply moved, for we had all been dazed and afflicted by the internecine struggle.

As fellow members of the first Free State Senate, W. B. Yeats and Gogarty became close companions. Both showed much moral courage. Yeats defended divorce for the minority. When the sale of preventitives was forbidden, Gogarty pointed out dramatically that another method could be found in the cruet on the dining-room table. Few young husbands and wives caught his hint that a plug of wadding steeped in vinegar was an old Victorian device.

For many years, Gogarty only published his poems in small private editions, because a doctor would have been regarded with much suspicion by his fellow-doctors and his patients, even in Dublin, if it were known that he was a poet. With the encouragement, however, of his lofty friend in the Senate, he felt at last that he could venture to publish a book.

An Offering of Swans was a classical gesture of thanksgiving for his escape when captured at night by armed men. Pleading natural necessity, he unbuttoned at a wall, and then dived into the Liffey. Yeats declared that his new friend was one of the great lyric poets of the age and that challenge still remains. Certainly, in a small number of poems, now widely known, he achieved a Jacobean grace, discipline, felicity, which might well have been envied by his old friend and enemy, James Joyce. I recall the evening when he

spoke for me in his mocking, joyful way, the poem *After Galen* –
fortunately we were walking along the street and there was nothing
on which he could thump out the stresses. It was not until middle
age that I learned to appreciate its moral.

> Only the Lion and the Cock,
> As Galen says, withstand Love's shock.
> So, dearest, do not think me rude
> If I yield now to lassitude,
> But sympathize with me. I know
> You would not have me roar, or crow.

Despite his intimacy with his fellow wit and poet, Seumas
O'Sullivan, Padraic Colum and other writers, Gogarty, in his verse,
remained outside the Irish mode. He was too versatile merely to be
a literary man and, no doubt, he worked off much imaginative
energy and repressed feeling in many pursuits such as fast driving
and piloting a small airplane. When he had to make a forced landing
on an isle off Connemara, with Lady Heath, a wit remarked, 'He's
on his native heath at last.'

In his late 50's, Oliver Gogarty abandoned a lucrative practice
and became a professional man of letters: an act of great courage.
No doubt, the suppressed poet and writer was urged by ambition
and a wild desire to lay the lively ghost of Buck Mulligan. In a
succession of books, with rollicking titles, the ex-doctor set down
his reminiscences in an exuberant but rather massive prose. *Mad
Grandeur*, the first of his two novels, has a promising theme but
fails to recapture for us the eighteenth century of rakes and 'bucks'.
Oliver Gogarty's struggle in the United States as an elderly writer
must have been hard, and in his last years, he was poor. On his few
return visits to Dublin however, he seemed ageless, as handsome,
inconsequential and debonair as when I first met him.

V

Early in July 1922, a small group of idlers, women and children,
who had gathered outside a house near Church Street drew back
respectfully as a well-known Franciscan preacher knocked at the

door. Inside, members of the Legion of Mary were trying to persuade thirty-one young prostitutes to undertake an enclosed Retreat. The frightened girls, who had been taken from the brothels, believed that this was a Government plot to lock them up for life.

The owner of the house asked £4 a day for boarding and keeping the girls, so a special meeting of the Praesidium was held at the Headquarters in Myra House, Francis Street, to discuss ways and means, for it was necessary to keep the prostitutes together, in order to save them from further temptations. It proved difficult to find a convent for the Retreat: eventually, however, the Sisters of Charity in Baldoyle offered to give the Legion the use of their school, but not of the normal Retreat House. To avoid scandal, it was arranged that the party would be presented as a Sacred Heart Sodality from the City. Legionaries went, after the meeting, to Gorevan's in Camden Street to buy beds, mattresses, pillows, blankets, sheets and chamber pots.

On the morning of July 14th, a private bus was to leave from Myra House for Baldoyle at 11.30. Some hours earlier, a Franciscan from Adam and Eve's agreed to conduct the Retreat subject to the approval of his superiors. As the girls came out of Myra House, a huge crowd waiting in the street sang, 'Faith of our Fathers', while old women knelt down on the pavement reciting the Rosary. On the way to Baldoyle, the bus stopped at Burgh Quay, and in a few minutes the Franciscan arrived. He agreed to come, but refused to travel with the Magdalens. Soon afterwards, more brothels were entered and the whores taken away. So, with the connivance of the new Provincial Government, Night-town was closed.

On July 15th, the Legion approached Mr. Cosgrave, Minister for Local Government for assistance in finding somewhere to place the girls after the Retreat. He gave them a sympathetic hearing, got them to write out their request and undertook to present it to the Government which was meeting that evening. On the following morning – a Sunday – the Legionaries returned and were given a letter in the Minister's own handwriting, which allowed them the use, free of rent and taxes for three months, of a house in Harcourt Street, recently vacated by the Department for Local Government. This is now Sancta Maria House. There was a good deal of discussion in the Legion about the inadvisability of taking a house which was in too good a neighbourhood. Attempts were made to get somewhere else and a message was sent to Baldoyle to prevent the girls from leaving there at the appointed time on the Monday morning. It proved impossible to find alternative accommodation, and on Monday afternoon, delegates went to the Department for Local Government for the key. From Mr. MacCarron, the Secretary, they received a cheque for £25. They had only just returned to the house, when the girls, who had not got the message, arrived by the bus. They were brought across the road to the Municipal Art Gallery and waited there for two hours while the house was being cleaned up. The rooms were unfurnished and so the Legionaries hurried down Golden Lane, by St. Patrick's Park and Engine Alley to Myra House. Despite the protests of the caretaker, they removed the furniture which was the property of the Society of St. Vincent de Paul. Later the Society presented it to the Legion of Mary with a cheque for £5. Meanwhile, the beds, mattresses, blankets, sheets and chamber pots had been brought to the house in Harcourt Street.

Of the 23 girls who attended the Retreat, three were married in a few months, one became engaged, two had to go to hospital, two returned to their home, employment was found for five, eight remained at the new hostel, two went back to a life of sin. Two, who were Protestants, were received into the Catholic Church, one in August, the other in September.

Fourteen

FEW REALIZE NOWADAYS that after the First World War there was an astonishing change in women's fashions: the era of the low neck and the short skirt had come. Every Sunday, in the sermon after the Gospel, the Dublin clergy denounced the immodesty of the new female dress and pointed out the danger to faith and morals, urging parents to assert their rightful authority and protect their young daughters. But the eloquence of Maynooth was in vain because women, having escaped from the flounces, lace petticoats, camisoles, whalebone and steel stays of corsets, long drawers, and woollen combinations of the Victorian age, could not be persuaded to get into them again, however chilled their legs might be. Even those who had thick ankles or stout calves were forced to reveal their drawbacks.

After some years, the newspapers were actually publishing advertisements and drawings of dainty lingerie – and old-fashioned readers did not dare to object. So the Church, with its male opportunism, accepted the inevitable change. Only in Dublin has ecclesiastical influence been successful and but in one instance. On Sundays and holy days of obligation, the Girl Pipers' Band, marching along briskly, with lifting kilts and bare knees, drew crowds of young and old men to the street corners. By the command of the Catholic Archbishop, the hems of the patriotic kilts had to be let down, two inches.

The city kerbs were a daily temptation: bad thoughts came round every corner and sped by, keeping to the left. Girls cycling past no longer wore the elastic ribbon sewn to the skirt as a protection against peeping Toms. Boldly they showed their kneecaps and when, on gusty days, their skirts blew up around them, men and boys could see two or three inches of bare thigh beneath the suspender. Others crouched in abandonment on the pillions of motor cycles, knobbling the rider with their knees, while their tightened skirts kept their bonny rounds from wobbling.

Later when I was in London, it was difficult during the summer to walk in Hyde Park admiring the flower plots and trees because a new fashion of open knickers had spread from Paris. Ladies on twopenny seat or free bench were a cause of temptation to men walking on the opposite side of the road. The passers-by were assailed only too quickly by Venus in her many manifestations: Cypria, Duplex, Amathusia, Paphia, Apostrophie, Urania, Pandimos, Acrene, Euphoea, Expolois – beyond the city, Phallommeda, Philommedis, Telessigama, Coluada, Colulis, Verticardia, Apaturia, Calea Ericyna, Etaira, Acidalia, Basilea Myrtea, Libertina, Mechanitis, patron of artificial means, Protectress of the Cautchouc Grove, Pontia, Marina, Limiesia, Epipontia, Pelagia, Pontogenea, Saligenia, Aligena, Thalassia, Anadyomene.

Suddenly that Paris fashion disappeared. Since the Second World War, young mothers have been pushing perambulators wearing mannish trousers, slacks, jeans, while girls sprawl on beaches in the gay bits of bikinis.

Despite the gloomy silence of the Church, a poet appeared daily in the streets of Dublin as a champion, endeavouring to save men from the immodest sights around them. Having been separated from his wife for many years, he may have endured the torments of the flesh. Portly, middle-aged, with abundant curly hair and black sombrero, he wore outside his waistcoat a sackcloth apron which reached down to his knees. Walking slowly along, Philip Francis Little stopped women, pointed accusingly at their low necks and short skirts, warning them in a loud voice of the flames of Hell. Mothers, shopping with their leggy little girls, dressed in pretty frocks and socks, did not escape his watchful eye and he implored them to think of the next world. He reproved even boys with short breeches and bare knees on their way home from school, and they stood before him, shame-faced and blushing to the ears. Terror spread from the Town Hall in Rathmines to the neighbouring squares and along the Terenure Road, so that whenever he appeared – a wrathful figure more than a hundred yards away – wives and girls fled round the nearest corner. Soon inside the tram, only men were to be seen for the women went on top in order that they might not be accosted by him.

II

One evening in the No. 15 tram, a drunken labourer was so surprised by the sackcloth that he leaned over and began to fumble it. I was sitting near the poet, and indignant at this insult to the Muse, I seized the annoying fellow by the shoulder as the tram slowed down on the canal bridge at Portobello, for the conductor was upstairs. Before he realized what was happening, I had hustled him off the step. With grave dignity, the poet raised his sombrero and said, 'Thank you, sir'.

On a blank wall in Rathmines, Philip Francis Little chalked denunciations of the British soldiers in the nearby barracks and the girls who went out walking with them at night time. Resenting this fuss, a few Tommies, with blackened faces, broke into his house, but he succeeded in escaping through a back door and ran down a lane. He reached the house of a friend, but that eminent citizen was afraid to shelter him. Once a large crowd stood outside his house in Rathmines, watching him below in the area. He was mounted on a step-ladder, holding up a cage and a lump of sugar in an attempt to coax back to its perch a canary which was clinging beyond his reach to the down pipe.

One day I met him on the Vico Road near Killiney and he stood talking to me in a deep musical voice. He ranged from Homer to St. Jerome and the early fathers of the Church, spoke of St. Paul and his wanderings, cited Dionysius, the Aeropagite, rolling the name voluptuously round his mouth, referred to his treatises on Mystical Theology and the Divine Names, discoursed at some length on the *Summa Theologicum* of Aquinas. I was held by his learned, erratic discourse and, as he rumbled down the centuries, I knew instinctively what was about to happen. Suddenly his expression became enraged; his eyes lit under bushy brows and raising his voice and stick, he denounced Henry VIII and all the spoils of the Reformation. I saw the faggoted flames of the auto-da-fé, heard the shrieks of heretics bound among them, heard, too, the wicked shouting of St. Dominic as he incited the massacre of the Albigenses. In the middle of the tirade, I stole away. Half a mile off, I passed two small girls talking gravely at the corner of the hill road that led to Killiney village.

'And he was very fat,' said the elder, as if she were repeating a nursery rhyme, 'and he had on him a big black hat.'

As I looked down at the narrow strait between Dalkey Island and the shore, it seemed to me that I had detected the last tiny ripple made by that ancient Irish water serpent, the *Great Piast*, on its way round our coast to the Shannon Estuary.

III

Philip Francis Little published a large collection in 1915 under the title *Thermopylae and Other Poems*. There is an odd take-it-or-leave-it foreword:

> The aim that all we poets have in writing is of pleasing ourselves, which is the object each one has when he is sneezing.

Most of the longer pieces are classical in theme, but Philip Francis Little shows no awareness in them of the kind of verse that others were writing in this country at the time. Occasionally he ventured into the Irish history of our schoolbooks. His poems are strangely unequal and his other self prompted him to trundle into heavily humorous poems, which are dire in their effect. Despite all this, there are unexpected delights in his academic work, lines which have the breadth and rich imagery of the Elizabethan age. They will remind some of Thomas Lovell Beddoes in *Death's Jest Book* and of Charles Wells in *Joseph and his Brethren*. Here is an example from one of his best poems, 'The Lighthouse-keeper.'

> In the inert cold air
> incessant snow toils on, erecting those
> enormous glaciers green, between whose horns
> dilated the great stars stand, tremulous,
> where mammoth caves, dusted with adamant,
> kennel the sea lion's litter.

And how imaginative is the adjective 'unreal' in the following lines:

> the startled heron, lifting her unreal
> and languid body from her pasturage.

107

Equally exact is the description of the wild coast flowers in the following passage:

> In such a tract, untenanted save by the grey
> and cindery smock-weed, and the flickering, blue
> sea-poppy, have I watched, marking the sweet,
> sweet tender notes, the sea-bird spends across
> those flat and squalid commons. Sweet were they!
> So sweet, if half so sweet, pipeth the lone,
> wild Tartar herdsman to the Evening Star.

Sad to relate, Dr. Sigerson, his fellow-poet, pointed out at the time that these plants are purely imaginary and so will not be found in any book on botany.

Fifteen

I

ONE EVENING, at about 5 o'clock, I happened to be on my way through the Coombe, by grocery store, dairy, bird-shop, huckster shops with sweets, bottles of fizz, coal blocks and turf. I stopped, as was my habit, to marvel at the thick stonewall, twenty-five feet in height, which hides the Convent and Chapel of the Sisters of the Holy Faith from the noise of the slums around them and the bad language of drunken men and women on Saturday nights at closing-time, staggering from the five public houses at the four corners I passed – Clanbrassil Street, Kevin Street, Patrick Street, the Coombe.

I heard the sharp clink of boot-metal coming along the pavement and, looking back, saw about thirty small orphans clad in warm grey clothes, marching along, led briskly by their Bible teacher. They had come, I had no doubt, from the neighbouring Protestant institution known as the Birds' Nest. Suddenly from the lanes and alleys darted ragged urchins, in delight; and running along in the gutter, they yelled at their traditional foes:

'Effing bastards! Swaddlers! Effing bastards!'

The orphans marched along in grim silence and even after they had passed the corner of Francis Street and were approaching the Catholic Church, I could still hear those opprobious taunts in the distance.

I wondered whether the poet, James Stephens, had known the same mockery as a child, when he marched through the streets with other foundlings. His twisted frame, goitrous throat, rickety limbs were due, no doubt, to malnutrition in infancy. He never spoke of his childhood though a glimpse may be had in that stark tale, *Hunger.* Often he would say, in his whimsical way that when he was a child he used to chase the ducks in St. Stephen's Green to steal bits of bread from them. He may have been rescued and

109

brought up in an institution for waifs and strays. He was a clerk in a solicitor's office in Dublin when A.E. discovered him, already starting to write poems, articles, for Arthur Griffith's periodical *Sinn Féin*. James Stephens was strange and dwarf-like in appearance, with a large head. An American artist, who illustrated a collection of Irish sagas, depicted him effectively as the Chief Druid, Cathva. Katherine Tynan once said to me that Padraic Colum had a look of wonder in his eyes like that of a young man going into a wood: James Stephens had the mysterious look of a young man coming out of a wood. The little man sat lightly, jigging and jerking, and I often thought that at any moment he might pop up on the back of his chair, the chimney-piece, or the top of the nearest sofa. Perhaps this was due to those apprentice years in which he sat on a high stool in an office. His wonderful fantasy, *The Crock of Gold*, might have come from nowhere, but F. R. Higgins once showed me a copy of *The Centaur* by Algernon Blackwood, which he had picked up on one of the book stalls at the corner of Aston Quay for a few pence. The name of James Stephens was written on the fly-leaf, in his own handwriting and the margins were full of his notes. Doubtless, that mythological escapade of ancient Greece, the thunder of centaur hooves on mountain sides and in groves around small temples, had inspired him. The last chapter, in which the Sidhe assembles on Kilmashogue, owes much to the vision of Red Hugh O'Donnell on Slieve Gullion in Standish O'Grady's historical novel, *The Flight of the Earls*. I fancy that A.E. must have read that passage out to him as he did to me at his house at 17 Rathgar Avenue, late at night amid a cloud of pipe tobacco smoke.

F. R. Higgins told me how one Sunday night, on his way to A.E.'s house, he was puzzled by a small bundle moving along past the lampposts. As he came near, he realized, much to his embarrassment, that the bundle was James Stephens, wrapped in a large French cavalry officer's cloak, which he had brought back with him from Paris. The little fellow must have realized soon the ridiculous figure he cut for no one else has mentioned seeing him so arrayed. Later Eamonn De Valera wore a cloak around him like Dan O'Connell, the Liberator, during his electoral campaign in Kerry, but his staff were always mislaying it. However, in the early 'thirties a photograph of the Taoiseach, cloaked, on horse-back, reviewing the Irish army, appeared in the newspapers. It happened to be a day of rain and mist so that in the photographs he appeared to be wearing merely a heavy waterproof cape.

My first visit to James Stephens in his flat at the top of a house in Fitzwilliam Street was my last. The room was full of people chatting and I found myself beside a strange-looking elderly man, dressed in neat black and pallid of face. He began to tell me in a slow, trance-like voice how much he admired the writings of the poet. Suddenly I was caught by the shoulder and hurried across the room by James Stephens. 'That fellow is a terrible bore,' he confided to me. 'He comes every Thursday and we don't know how to get rid of him.' I clenched my toes nervously in my shoes for I feared that the bore might overhear our conversation and I watched him across the room all that evening, sitting bolt upright, staring into space. The experience was so unnerving that I did not visit the flat again. Sometimes I met the bore in the street, and feeling sorry for him, I saluted him in a friendly way but never stopped to be talked to.

When Stephens was Curator of the National Gallery, I called one afternoon to see him in his office. He sat behind an enormous desk and after a few minutes of talk produced mysteriously a thick type-script from a drawer, held it up and told me that it was the first part of the prose epic which he was writing, *The Cattle Raid of Cuailgne.* He looked as if he were about to perch on the edge of the desk, then suddenly he clapped the typescript back into the drawer again, his egg, his beloved treasure. After twenty minutes or so, A.E. who was on his way home from Plunkett House, called for him. We walked past the railings of Merrion Square, the two arguing over politics. James Stephens was, like myself, a follower, at that time of the anti-Treaty party. 'Up De Valera,' he piped defiantly, and recited a triolet which he had written to the leader of the Irregulars.

II

Later, when I had gone to live in London, I met James Stephens one day in the Strand and he asked me to come out and see him at his house in Wembley some time. On a wintry afternoon I set out from Chelsea on the long journey by Underground and bus. When I got off the bus I had to walk a mile in the bitter cold and darkness, so I looked forward pleasantly to a hot cup of tea and conversation. On the right, at the top of a gradient, I came to a place which a passer-by told me was called Blackbird Farm. There was no tillage, only a wood, half cut down, a muddy unfinished road, builders' sheds, a row of new bungalows. I came at last to the right number in the row and saw a light in one of the windows but the latch of the garden gate was so stiff that I could not raise it. I stood puzzled for a moment; then stepped over the small gate, wondering if the small poet vaulted over it. Mrs. Stephens opened the door and told me that her husband was in London. She did not know when he would return. I explained politely that I had come all the way from Chelsea and that he had asked me to call at any time. I realized that it had been foolish of me not to 'phone or write. The hot cup of tea disappeared as she closed the door and I had to make my way through the mud of the building site again. I learned later that there had been many marital rows and the poet often spent a day in London, roaming the streets in solitude and misery. Perhaps I had come there on one of those days of quarrel.

III

Once, at an exhibition of paintings by Jack B. Yeats in a Bond Street gallery, I met James Stephens. As I was staring blankly at a large picture, all blankness of blackness with a red patch in the middle, a woman friend asked Stephens what it was about. He avoided that tricky question and, pretending to have a scissors in his hand, darted near the canvas. 'Look at the wonderful texture,' he exclaimed. 'I'd love to snip off a square inch of it and if I did so, here or there, that corner or this, the texture would still be the same.' Suddenly, we heard the voice of the artist above our lowered heads. 'When I was a boy in Sligo,' he was saying, 'I was on the bridge one dark night. An old man stopped to light his pipe. As he cupped his hands, I saw a tiny glowing world – and then the match went out.'

His voice was so quiet that it became hypnotic and as he described the little rite, we saw the match light up and that tiny glowing world among the shadows on the bridge as the old man puffed at his pipe. Then the match went out and we were staring into the blackness of the picture and the artist had disappeared among the crowd.

112

IV

A few weeks before his sudden death, I met James Stephens and his wife at a lunch given to us in the Café Royal, by our friend, Philip Sayers. As we drank light wine, sipped our brandy and smoked Havana cigars, the poet capered gaily. Never had I heard him talk so well. We lingered there after the waiters had cleared the table and the other lunchers had gone back to their offices, and yet I can remember nothing of all that brilliant conversation owing to the haze of my mind. Mrs. Stephens seemed to approve of me for in a lull she invited me to come to their house on the following Thursday. Stephens had a wonderful range of subjects, for he had lectured many times throughout the United States and for years was part-Librarian to a millionaire who had a palace in Los Angeles, and a large one, it is said, on the Berkeley Hills. The position was really a sinecure, and the Irish poet was mediaeval court jester at his patron's table.

To my surprise, when I arrived at Wembley, I found myself in the shopping centre of a large suburb and spent twenty minutes wandering down side-streets and crescents before I found the bungalow which I had seen years before – and this time the latch yielded easily to my hand. In the small back drawing-room were several guests and I could see through the window a row of apple-trees planted, no doubt, at the time I had ventured beyond the vanished Blackbird Farm on that winter's evening long ago. I sat on a cushioned divan with Mrs. Stephens close to me, telling me of the years they had spent in Paris and of her illustrious descent from the French Court. She was still a pretty, petite woman and I remembered that she was said to have been an equestrienne in a travelling circus, and I could see her there in tights and tinsel. Opposite was James Stephens talking vividly and I longed to hear what he was saying, but his wife talked on. At last there was a respectful silence – the poet was about to tell a story.

'Once upon a time three hermits decided to retire to a remote part of Connaught. After a year of silence and meditation, one of them said, 'It's very quiet down here.' After a year had passed the second hermit answered him, 'Yes'. At the end of another year the third hermit exclaimed, 'There's too much talk in this place, I'm leaving.'

Everyone was delighted by the traditional tale, but I remembered with embarrassment that A.E. had told it to me one evening in Rathgar. In his later years, James Stephens played the part of sage and owed much to the example of A.E. whom he always reverenced as the Master. So I was careful to avoid his eye after he had told the story.

Before we left, James Stephens and his wife both retired into the kitchenette. We could hear the clink of glasses and the rattle of ice. Then he served us impishly with so potent a cocktail, that Norah Hoult, the novelist, and I hurried back to town so elated that we spent the rest of the evening drinking beer in a public house near Marble Arch in order to quench our burning thirst.

Sixteen

I

LT. COL. MEYLER, D. S.O., had his offices in a side street near Victoria Station and it seemed strange to me that this distinguished, grey-haired solicitor should spend his hours in so drab a neighbourhood. His gallantry in the First World War assured me of his respectability and his name had been recommended to me by our family solicitor in Dublin. I saw Lt. Col. Meyler only once or twice despite my frequent visits to the office, for he had put my case in charge of his confidential clerk, an astute young man of foreign appearance, whose face was pitted disagreeably as a result of smallpox. I had saved a few hundred pounds, having decided to take a divorce action in the hope of ending a registry office marriage which had lasted only ten days. Margaret was unwilling to release me and there was no chance of a nullity suit.

After the usual delay of many months, the date of the hearing was fixed. The evening before the case, I was puzzled by the fact that I had not met our Counsel. The next morning, a quarter of an hour before we entered the Court, the brief was handed to a junior barrister, who glanced down it hastily before asking me a few questions. The case itself, which was heard by Lord Merrivale, was as hasty. I knew that the Judge had been a high official in Dublin Castle during the Black-and-Tan regime: it was believed that his peerage was a reward for services. Counsel for the defence was a well-known K.C., who, with much skill, questioned my intentions in coming to reside in England. I thought that the Judge looked down at me with distaste from the bench and I realized that my case was lost.

To escape from misery for a few days, I hurried to an acquaintance of mine, an Indian doctor who had been struck off the medical register and lived in a slum street of Fulham. He gave me a bottle which must have contained a powerful bromide for,

115

whenever I took a dose, I drifted into a far-away carefree region. As a dear friend endeavoured to console me on my divan, her voice faded from the attic studio in Redcliffe Road. The rattle of delivery vans, the cheerful street-cry of the coal-man and the muffin-man were as distant.

The poet, F. R. Higgins, sent me a telegram urging me to stay with him in Connemara for some weeks. He had left Dublin when verse was retreating before the excitement of prose. Brinsley MacNamara, and the new short-story writers, Liam O'Flaherty, Frank O'Connor, Seán O'Faoláin, Peadar O'Donnell, were all realists, interested in the era of violence. Higgins was editing a small trade paper and persuaded the printing firm of Thom's to let him produce it from a remote part of Connaught at a salary of £3 a week – not much, but the poet was frugal and his wife, May, shared his courage. So he moved furniture and books to a cottage near the shore of Lough Conn opposite Mount Nephin, mentioned in so many of the Gaelic love-songs which have come down from the seventeenth and eighteenth centuries.

I returned to Dublin, bought a secondhand Peugeot Coupé with what was left of my savings and spent a week learning to drive on a road with dips and sharp corners under the old lead workings of Carrickmines, near our home at Killiney.

II

On a sunny morning, I drove from the city along the Liffey Valley, past the eighteenth-century mansions and demesnes near the slopes of Knockmaroon, past Maynooth Castle from which Silken Thomas had ridden out in rebellion. Exhilarated by a newly won skill, I drove by the great central bog of Allen for several hours and could only see the long empty road ahead.

Somewhere by the edge of the brown bog, I have seen a tiny town of wooden huts. Opposite it, is a new limestone church, almost as large as a Cathedral and a quarter of a mile away a new Cinema. Despite these attractions, men could not be persuaded to leave the city for the project of reclaiming the boglands, started by Bord na Mona. Today strange machines like saurians move slowly along the horizon and for gleaming miles can be seen the ridges of cut turf

116

protected by plastic coverings. The fuel, which had given warmth during the winter and wet summers to country folk for centuries, is burned rapidly in the furnaces of factories and will have been exhausted in fifty years. The wildlife, so well described by Lord Dunsany in several of his books, has gone.

About two o'clock, having eaten my ham sandwiches, I was going up a long gradient in second gear when I heard strange groans. From under the bonnet came a smell of burning rubber and oil. I got out hastily, fearing that the infernal machine was about to explode. Nothing happened, however, and after a short time, the engine cooled, so I ventured on cautiously until I came to the bridge over the Shannon at Easkey, and loitered by the waters.

Towards evening, I reached the small town of Foxford and saw the river gardens sloping towards the River Moy which F. R. Higgins had known as a youngster. I drove by Lough Cuillin, catching glimpses of the glittering creeks, the wooded islets dark against the evening sky. Then, consulting my map and making enquiries from a few men by a stone-heap, I went slowly along the shore-road of Lough Conn, opposite Mount Nephin, but in my eagerness, I missed the boreen down to Brackwansha. Vainly, I tried to turn on the narrow road, for I had not learned to reverse. Several men came from the fields and for a quarter of an hour tried to push the small car around. Then, a young Mayo man solved the problem. He opened the gate of a field: I drove slowly around on the clayey soil, and came out in the right direction. Unfortunately, in my haste while passing a cottage, some distance away, I drove over a goose. I came back the next day to pay for the loss of it but the man and his wife would not take any money.

The cottage in which F. R. Higgins and his wife settled down in the previous autumn was new and had been occupied by a school-teacher. It had a kitchen with an open hearth and the usual three-legged pot suspended from a hook. There was also a pleasant parlour, its bookshelves filled gaily.

After supper, Fred and I wandered along the pebbly shore in the twilight, beyond shadowy bushes, watching the reflection of Mount Nephin, mysterious as Venusburg on the still water. He pointed out the stepping stones across a stream over which, according to tradition, the Welshmen of Tirawley had stumbled, when their enemies offered them the grim choice between being blinded or

117

losing their manhood. He quoted that powerful ballad for which Samuel Ferguson might have drawn a hint from a stanza form used by Thomas Campbell:

> Scorna Boy, the Barrett's bailiff,
>   Lewd and lame,
> To lift the Lynotts' taxes when he came,
> Rudely drew a young maid to him;
> Then the Lynotts rose and slew him;
> And in Tubber-na-Scorney threw him.
>   Small your blame,
>   Sons of Lynott!
> Sing the vengeance of the Welshmen of Tirawley.

Ferguson, however, states in a note that *Clochan-na-n'all*, the Blindmen's stepping-stones is on the Duvowen River about four miles beyond Crossmolina, at the north-west corner of Lough Conn.

III

On the following morning, which was a Sunday, I was surprised to see strolling along the road, past the low stone walls, companies of young ladies, dressed in fine frocks, all wearing rayon stockings and high-heeled shoes. At a distance, they seemed as unreal as women of the Sidhe. I saw no cars, and wondered, but said nothing. On Monday morning, the languid strollers had all become rough girls in big boots, working in the little fields, or clattering with buckets from the nearby clachan to the well. Fred explained to me that their sisters, cousins, send them their spare dresses and other finery from the United States. They, too, were hoping to emigrate as soon as they had saved up their steerage fare. Most of them wore bandages around their cheeks because there was an epidemic of toothache, due, no doubt, in those low-lying acres around the lake, to the damp and evening mist. Promptly, I got a sympathetic toothache and failed to dodge pain for more than a few minutes with oil of cloves which was sold in a huckster shop a few miles away. I had to wait for the lady dentist, who came to Ballina, was only in attendance once a week. On the particular day we drove the six miles into the town. I looked nervously at her slight wrist, all the more so because the girl seemed hesitant. But she was used to the big teeth of the local farmers. In a few seconds, with remarkable skill, she had extracted the molar.

Clocks tick slowly in the West and we were usually eating our breakfast, which often consisted of fried slices of goose-egg as thick as pancakes, when the postman left his cycle at the gate and came in for a chat by the turf fire. Outside, I could see through the bay-window the sloe blossoming for miles along the narrow roads around the lake: exotic, Japanese, Mount Nephin, though without its winter snows, was Fujiyama.

Fred had an old scarlet-coloured Citroen car. He was a skilful driver, though a rapid one. So I was not too anxious as we whirled past the miles of sloe blossom, feeling that we were safely mounted on Pegasus. Later he wrote his ballad, *The Flowering Sloe*:

> My darling walks by with lace at each hand,
> In shoes of dim buckles, O watch my love stand:
> At bull-ring or races he makes the best show,
> While his beauty makes light of the flowering sloe.

A couple of nights after my arrival, I tasted poteen for the first time. Bottles of the illicit spirit were kept well hidden in common ground by the road-sides. After darkfall, we went down to a cottage where a raffle was being held by an elderly couple to raise some money for the rent. I was brought through the kitchen, where boys and girls were dancing, into the bedroom. There, in accordance with custom, the Woman of the House took from the cupboard a large bottle and poured out a cupful of poteen. Being determined to be manly, I drank it off and, to my surprise, was possessed by so great a glow of energy that I dashed wildly into the kitchen again, grabbed a buxom wench as firmly as though she were the melodeon, and bounced around with her, almost knocking down the swinging lamp overhead. Then, the effect of the liquor went and I was completely sober once more.

Fred told me sadly that the traditional lore had gone, all except a few political ballads of Young Ireland and the Fenian years. Along the Ox Mountains, however, there was still legendary lore and on the next Sunday night, wild strangers came down from the

119

hill-farms to a neighbouring cottage. Among them was the local beauty, proud, with a head of black ringlets. When I tried later that night to steal a kiss, she pushed my face away in play, smilingly, but such was her strength that it might have been the hoof of a mare, iron shoe and all. Word of the petting parties fashionable then in New York seemed to have reached this remote countryside, for at midnight the paraffin lamp was extinguished. The courting, as often as not, began with a struggle, but these powerful girls suddenly yielded after a few minutes, realizing, no doubt, that townsmen had not sufficient strength to vie with their country muscles. This happy struggle could have been a survival of the ancient marriage by capture. Old customs described by Lady Wilde in a neglected book on Irish folklore, still lingered by Lough Conn. Fred told me of a marriage rite in which he had taken part when the elders were away at the monthly fair in Ballina. He and a dark-eyed, gamesome girl were chosen for the ceremony of the bedding of groom and bride: while the others were laughing and singing songs, they had some quiet fun to themselves between the sheets.

In the darkness, we hugged, fondled, kissed, long into the night. Hands stole beyond holy medals to warm, plump breasts, crept slyly along firm thighs, but these girls knew how to guard their skirts. We exchanged couples and the kisses, hugs, squeezes, ticklings, daring pinches, playful slaps, began again until once more knees were firmly crossed. Our willing partners, as they shared longer kisses and sighs with us, knew only too well that their parents were wise in litigation, and were always ready to take an action for seduction.

The nearest chapel was several miles away and so the clergy rarely darkened the half-door of the cottages by the lake. Once, at Sunday Mass, after the sermon, the Parish Priest denounced all the congregation and flung from the pulpit, as if each coin were accursed, the thirty or more silver pieces which made up the season's offerings. So the Devil was busy among the bushy hollows at night. Young men told enviously of the farrier from the Ox Mountains whom no young girl could resist, so potent was this legendary blackguard in middle-age. The young curate of a remote parish was friendly with a married woman who lived forty miles away. Once a week he sent his man in a car to bring her to his sight. The people wondered, but remained silent about the couple, respecting their plight, as though they were lovers in an old Gaelic song.

Once a week, we drove to Ballina for the week's provisions. In a public house there, were several bottles of Benedictine. We drank it by the tumbler-full for the barman only charged us a shilling; believing that this was profitable. We avoided the jetty near the Cathedral where the salmon were brought ashore. A large drag-net was used, so that none could escape, and the struggling fish were bludgeoned brutally and expertly.

On a fair day, as we came towards Ballina, we saw a saloon car, half a mile away, rocking from one side of the road. Suddenly, it tumbled into the dyke. A number of carts came in sight, and the drivers standing up in them, shook their reins, carefully keeping their heads turned away. Horrified by such inhumanity, I asked Fred the reason as he drove as fast as he could to the place of the accident. He explained that it was due to traditional fear of the law; the cart-men did not want to be summoned to court as witnesses. Fully expecting that the overturned car might burst into flames at any moment, we got out and dashed towards it. The door slowly opened sideways and a local Councillor crawled out. Staggering to his feet, he answered our anxious enquiries with a contemptuous question: 'What the hell do yiz want here?'

A south-westerly gale was blowing across the lake on the day that Fred had to drive to Foxford with the copy for *Oil and Colour*, which he edited from his country retreat. His wife and I accompanied him as ballast to prevent the car from being overturned on one of the bog causeways. Soon we were racing the train and the Editor had barely time to hand the bulky envelope to the signal-man at the level crossing.

We ranged the countryside in sun and shower, following the images which the poet had found here and there:

Just telling each hour by the change of colour
On the mountains of Mayo.
We lingered quietly in Killala:

A town that yawned as the French marched through it
And never awoke since then!

We drove along the western shore past Glen Nephin, and came

to Crossmolina which is mentioned by Synge.

We were on our way to the wilds of Erris, where *The Playboy of the Western World* is set. Across the boglands, we saw the Moving Mountain and stopped for a few minutes to skitter stones along the parapet of the Musical Bridge, on which, with patience, one might learn to play a tune, faintly tinkling as a dulcimer. Along the coast, beyond the last small town of Belmullet, forty miles from the nearest railway, the rocks seemed to be of silver.

Southwards, we explored the country through which Raftery, the blind poet, wandered before the years of the Famine. He has described his yearly itinerary in a poem translated by James Stephens:

> In Claremorris I would stop a night and sleep with decent
>   men,
> And then go on to Balla just beyond and drink galore,
> And next to Kiltimagh for a visit of about a month, and then
> I would only be a couple of miles away from Ballymore.

Whisky has only two rhymes in the English language – 'frisky' and 'risky' so we have had in the past a lot of stage-Irish songs on the subject. F. R. Higgins was the first poet to write about the national drink as others wrote about wine. He wrote not of the wealthy distilleries, but of the outlawed spirit, the traditional comforter and medicine of poor people in damp glens near the Atlantic coast, first brought to us, according to legend, by Saint Patrick.

> So we, with the last dark men,
> Left on the rock grass,
> May brazen grey loneliness
> Over a poteen still
> Or crowd on the bare chapel floor
> Hearing late Mass,
> To loosen that hunger
> Broken land can never fill.

The third last line of that stanza is mine, for the poet had written ignorantly, 'receiving the Mass', and I hastened to correct that

Protestant error! The very word 'still' fascinated him. So he wrote in *An Old Air*:

> 'Then live with me, man, and I will give you
> The run of twelve hills with a still in each'
> Her eyes were craving that rainy evening,
> While a gentle air was in her speech.

The Royal Irish Constabulary winked and took their share of the illegal spirit, being content to keep the poteen-making within reasonable limits. In the Free State, the new Civic Guards watched with German binoculars for the tell-tale smoke. Higgins kept his bottle, like everyone else, hidden in common land by the roadside. When it was empty, we hired a boat and rowed for several miles down the lake to an island, with a 'street' of white-washed cottages on it. We sat in one of the cottages for an hour or more, drinking tea and eating soda-bread with currants in it, while a boatman rowed out to an islet beyond one of the wooded creeks. At dusk, our boat stole homeward again. We were, of course, law-breakers, but we had another bottle – for six shillings. Now the islanders have to get their medicine in the local dispensary.

III

After three weeks, I was unable to endure the nightly kisses, hugs, squeezes, pinches, tickles, fumblings, longer kisses and sighs. Many a Celtic saint had his *Virgo subinducta* to tempt him in the small hours, a tub of cold water nearby, into which he could jump if necessary. Such a cure was too drastic. So I drove off to stay in Healy's Hotel at Pontoon, a narrow hilly ridge between the two lakes, along which wild goats roamed. I listened at night to the talk of a few anglers or read again in the large volume of *Silva Gadelica* the story of Saint Cellach. He was King of Connaught but refused the crown and retired to one of the islands in Lough Conn. Fearing that he might weary of his life as a hermit, his successor, King Guaire bribed three of the pupils, whom Cellach had taught at Clonmacnoise to murder him. He begged them to spare him for a night, and they put him in the hollow of an oak, and kept guard over him. At dawn he composed a poem, which is Franciscan in tone. Here are the opening stanzas in the literal version by Seán O'Faoláin.

> Welcome, pale morning
> That cometh on the floor of my little cell,
> Welcome be the sender
> Of the ever-young victorious morning.
>
> Pale, proud morning,
> Sister of the pure sun;
> Welcome be the pale morning
> Lighting for me my little breviary.

I sent a telegram to London and followed by steam. Avril was waiting on the divan in my attic studio, as I hurried from the underground. Pleased and somewhat surprised by my unwonted impatience, she consoled me and soon I was hidden among her Plantagenet kisses.

IV

In his last book, F. R. Higgins included a humorous poem called *The Boyne Walk*, an account of a day's outing with the Westmeath novelist, Brinsley MacNamara. Both writers had the traditional secretiveness of the countryman. On one occasion, I saw MacNamara in Brunswick Street, escorting a married woman with whom he was said to be very friendly. When he caught sight of me, he said something to her and hurried into a small tobacconist's shop until I had gone by. Some months later, on a Sunday morning, he was standing on the top step of the house in Waterloo Road where he lodged, prayer-book in hand. His wife and child were already at the gate. On seeing me, he said a few words to his wife and retreated into the house. Much amused, I waited at a distant corner. In half a minute he came out again, looked cautiously up and down the road, and then went down the steps.

Brinsley MacNamara was the first of our realistic novelists and his book *The Valley of the Squinting Windows* caused a local sensation. It showed the influence of that powerful novel, *The House with Green Shutters* by George Douglas Browne. It was a sombre study of the effect of malicious gossip and ended on a note of tragedy. The inhabitants of his native village in Westmeath concluded that it was about them and promptly took their revenge by boycotting the National School in which his father was the Principal teacher. On his dismissal, the elderly man took legal action against the clerical manager. He lost the case, for no Irish jury will give a verdict against a priest, however cruel or unchristian his conduct. So the unfortunate young writer had to support his parents for the rest of their lives. During the Civil War he was forced by poverty to take a secret post in the Censor's Office of the new Provisional Government. One evening, he happened to pass me in Lincoln Place, guarded by two formidable gunmen. A brief poem which I had written about Liam Mellowes, one of the Republican leaders, had just appeared in an illegal news-sheet.

'That was a good poem of yours,' he shouted truculently, 'but not its sentiment.' I thought it safer not to reply.

The novels of Brinsley MacNamara were written in a clumsy prose which, unwittingly, expressed the slow, tortuous mind of the folk of the Midlands. Later he published *The Various Lives of Marcus Igoe,* a remarkable experiment, which has never had its due. Equally neglected are his short stories, tender and humorous, subtle in their quietness and hinting. They are outside the talkative, exhibitionist mode of our other short-story writers.

Brinsley MacNamara was a tall, handsome man, powerful in appearance, slow and heavy in his speech. But I remember how his voice crooned gently over every word one evening in the Palace Bar as he told us – after several drinks – one of his short stories. It was an idyll of young love, symbolized delicately by a wild swan's nest in the sedge of the River Boyne. His later short stories showed a further development. *The Three Mad Schoolmasters* is a realistic extravaganza, as fine in its own way as that well-known story *The Weaver's Grave* by Scumas O'Kelly.

MacNamara had been an Abbey actor for a few years before he began to write and so acquired a practical knowledge of stage-craft. He wrote several successful comedies, the best of them being *Look at the Heffernans*, and one tragedy which might have been a masterpiece. *Margaret Gillan*, in the first version had ended with a dumb cry of loneliness and despair. Unfortunately, the Manager of the Abbey Theatre, Lennox Robinson, persuaded the playwright to use a violent ending. The distraught, middle-aged woman kills the man who has tormented her, using her carving knife with remarkable skill. When I had read the play for a London publisher, I begged Brinsley to return to the original ending but failed in my attempt.

On a November evening, I found myself by chance in the company of Brinsley MacNamara and a few friends at Mooney's Bar in Piccadilly Circus. After closing-time, we went to a nearby nightclub. The novelist slumped into a chair – for Guinness is good for sleep – and our efforts to rouse him were in vain. Several pretty girls, amused by his snores, came over to help us. They kissed him gaily, slapped his face gently, pulled his ears, pinched, tickled, caressed him, but he slumbered on. About two a.m. Guinness released him from its trance. We brought him to the main Lyons Restaurant, where he was revived by strong tea, bread and butter, a pair of kippers. As he was fond of women, we did not tell him of the kisses, pinches and leg-pulls which he had not been in a condition to enjoy.

Seventeen

I

IT WAS PLEASANT TO BE YOUNG in the Age of Dunlop when so many rode out on stale air through the fresh air of the suburbs – to the Beyond. I pedalled along the remote roads of the West, changed gear, pushed up steep hills, free-wheeled down steeper hills, glided with the Atlantic wind against my shoulders. One day, in early September, I cycled to Ballyshannon to see the memorial on the town bridge to the poet, William Allingham, and the ancient Falls of Assaroe. The waters are stricken now because of the ugly dam built for the new hydroelectric schemes. I was soon coasting back along the road to Sligo, the south-west wind blowing through my hair as the clouds moved towards the nearby mountains. The sun clouded, showers came, went, suddenly. Yellow light swept once more across little fields and their rocks. As I was going swiftly downhill, an old woman hurried to a cottage gate and her voice was blown about my ears, so that I could only catch its words with difficulty: 'Put your cap on, sonny, or you'll catch cold'. Her motherly concern surprised me but I was going too fast to stop and could only wave a greeting to her. It seemed to me, as I swept southward, that Nature itself had shown this kindly concern for me. About ten miles farther on, I came to a rise and stopped for, of a sudden, I was, for the first time, in the Epic Age beside Fionn MacCumhail:

> He stood knee deep in ferns; boar-like, his eyes
> Glinting. He saw above the forest's verge
> The black blunt precipice of Gulban rear
> Skyward, the clouded mountain-tops and three
> Eagles in the high blue air like flies
> Flickering around a solitary peak.
> Below: the windy hillocks dropped to the sea –

A blue-green shadowed plain, and salt-white surge
Pawed round black capes.

On another occasion, I stayed for a week at Teelin in County
Donegal, because I wanted to see the cliffs of Slieve League. After
a meal of strong tea and herrings, I left the inn and, as I went down
the village street, I heard in the darkness the patter of steps. Half a
dozen youngsters ran beside me calling out in shrill tones: 'Tabhair
dom pinghin. Tabhair dom pinghin' (Gimme a penny)'.

It was the first time I had heard Irish spoken as a living language
– fittingly by bare-footed urchins – and I was thrilled by the sharp
syllables.

March winds blew every day and when I climbed to the last ridge
of Slieve League, I could only crawl a few yards along One Man's
path and peer at the ocean, two thousand feet below, where
sea-mews looked no bigger than their eggs.

Far and wide I wandered on to upper glens of rock and water,
dreaming of the Age of Epic. Wearing stout boots, with ashplant in
hand, compass in pocket, I climbed to the top of Carrantuohill,
Errigal, Lugnaquilla and other mountains. Once I met an old man
in a pass above Lough Inagh. While we sat under a boulder, he
talked to me of the twenty years which he had spent working in
several cities of America. The legendary past vanished. He droned
on. I was aware of the noise and rush of great cities. After that I
turned and went in the opposite direction whenever I saw an old
shepherd on the hills, lest he, too, had come back from the New
World.

II

Every summer, A.E. stayed for a month in a hillside cottage, a few
miles from Sheephaven, spending his days in reverie or in painting
pictures. Sometimes he went with his brushes and box of paints to
the cliff-house above Marble Strand where his friend, Hugh Law,
lived. He worked in the large studio there under a north light. He
had a remarkable power of visualization and when he returned to
Dublin, he spent the weekends at his easel, dipping his brushes into
memory. I was fascinated by the unearthly hues of those landscapes,

in which the May moon, pale as primrose, shone above the foam-edges along the strand where the vague forms of young girls could be seen.

A glimmer of dancing shadows,
A dovelike flutter of hands.

One evening, he suggested that I should visit north-west Donegal. Little did he guess that after a few adventures in the wilds there and on Tory Island, I would meet the Protestant Girl and cross the unseen border with her.

So, in the month of September, I travelled to Strabane, changed there to the single-track Donegal line. The small train, with its plain third-class carriages, went past bogland and mountain, rattling over the culvert bridges until we came to the station under the wooded ridge at Ards. I cycled along the hilly road for two and a half miles to the guest-house at Buttermilk Port, which was owned by a large cheerful lady and her dumpy sister. The fare was simple and the dessert always the same: blackberries and thick yellow custard. Often in the morning, when the other guests had gone out, I loitered in the austere parlour, with its ill-tuned piano, chairs and horsehair sofa, while a pretty young maid was scrubbing the floor. I picked out tunes on the piano, lest anyone should come in, stopping as often as I dared, to cuddle Peggy and clasp her firm breasts, while I snatched backward, teasing kisses. Then, to cool myself, I hurried out and swam in the small harbour.

In the afternoon, I wandered along the coast to Breaghy Head, staring down at the tide, fifty feet below, in the dangerous inland chasms. Near the headland were deep caves, radiant with iridescent hues. Once, at the entrance of a cave, I saw in the clear green water a huge lobster swimming slowly towards me. Stirred by an atavistic impulse, I thought cutely that I would wait quietly and then, when he was nearer, scoop him out of the water with a quick gesture. But another atavistic impulse stayed my hand. So, instead, I dipped my stick into the water. Immediately, the lobster gave it a mighty thwack with his tail and sped across the cave. Often, after that, I was awakened by the cave-echo of his thwack.

A week after my arrival, a south-westerly gale blew along the coast for several days and the flying sand prevented us from venturing out. I found myself back in the seventeenth century:

> Far waves came back at day
> To double their white dances,
> As though they were still breaking
> On rock. Low skies outran
> The rain: but Claremen played
> Backgammon in the house
> And squander of their crowns
> Was molten as the haze,
> Blowing from the foundries
> Of storm within the south.

On the third morning, the sand was laid and we could go out again.

III

The quay was always deserted when I looked out of the window at morning. The headland, across the bay, might be stretching darkly between driven clouds, or richly with green and blue acres if the cold sun were vigorous. But that tiny quay, hidden by a turn of the rocky Donegal coast, was always grey and bare, as though it had been boycotted even by the white cottages that sheltered behind the last hills. No tramp steamer, with its ragged smoke, had ever grumbled round the corner from the sea, and long since the bright shoals of herring had forgotten that bay.

But one morning the unexpected happened. I looked out of the window and there on the little quay, under the broken lee of the wall, a knot of men was around a fire. Even at that distance I knew by the awkwardness that these men were strangers. For in an unfamiliar neighbourhood our senses become primitive, and shoulder and limb guard themselves with a needless caution. I knew, too, without thinking, that these strangers had come suddenly from the sea, for who but castaways would build their fire on that uncharted quay and sit around it?

Without saying a word in the house, I stole out, and crossing the muffled sands of the sea-road dodged among the hillocks to spy upon the wonder. There was no ship's boat in the small harbour, for I knew all the old boats that wobbled there when the tide came back, as though they ached from lying on one side half the day. In the bay not even a sail was to be seen. In a puzzle I went round the old boat-shed that was always locked and came on a young seaman in a dark jersey who had drifted from the fire. He was hanging over a large log, hacking at it idly with a jack-knife. He met my excited enquiries with a dull look. But I got an odd word from him as he curled back the chips with his knife. His steamer had been wrecked off Torinis; the islanders had given the crew food and rowed them to the mainland. I found a few broken staves behind the shed, and followed at his heel to the fire, confident that his fellows would prove less taciturn.

But the rough, dark crew at the fire met my greeting with a nod or two, like men in a public house, who turn back to the counter when they have been interrupted. I began to feed the fire daringly, leaning a cunning ear here and there, for the seamen spoke an odd word now and again among themselves. But I could not catch what they were saying. At last a low-sized man, with a brown skin and large powerful hands, who seemed to be their leader, turned to me and asked in an expressionless tone: 'What part of the country is this?'

'Donegal,' I answered.

'How far's it to the nearest town?' he asked with more show of interest.

'About fifteen miles,' I replied, eager to talk. But he said no more.

'Maybe you're thinking of going there,' I suggested cutely.

'The Cap'n's gone there to report,' he said curtly, and lapsed into silence. I was abashed then and saw how foolish my curiosity had been. Shipwreck is only picturesque in town imaginings and in books. But, in reality, men are stunned and humiliated by sudden loss of their power, and, shelterless, they are aware, instinctively, of the ancient enmity of sky and rock. I crept away.

The cottages at the back of the hills were very quiet and watchful. There must be great gossip within.

'Wreck, begod,' said a boatman, thumbing his pipe at the turf fire, and stopping to look at me with pitying contempt, 'That's no wreck at all.'

So he explained that the owner of the wrecked vessel was

accustomed to send his rusty steamers on the rocks for the sake of the insurance money. I wondered how he knew so much about the shipowner who lived in Sligo or Limerick, but he thumped his knee with certainty. I remembered then the resentful looks of the seamen, their vague replies to me, the curt Glasgow tones.

The little crew was still huddled around its fire as I skirted carefully beyond the quay that evening, and made my way to a great hill that overlooked the ocean. Across the silver level of the Atlantic, I saw the fore of the island, clear and desolate in the sunset. But there was no sign of wreckage along the southward reef, and I felt triumphantly that I had found the seamen out in a lie. But a little foam was breaking brightly by itself, beyond the rocks, and in the dazzle, thin and tremulous as telegraph wires, I made out the masts of the sunken steamer.

It was darkfall when I came to the quarry top, above the road, and far below I saw the glow of the fire and the melancholy figures of the men, but the quay itself was merry with shadows. In the night, the folk were watching as I watched, shy and suspicious of the intruders, and wondering, no doubt, why the captain was still missing.

Suddenly the road, hidden below, rang with hooves and the brisk jingle of an outside car. Abruptly an immense voice rose in the dark, roaring and rejoicing in a strange song beyond the latitude of tune. No married man in that quiet land, however drunken, had ever given the rein, and bawled so fearlessly, so shamelessly, to the stars. I wondered who the devil it could be. The galloping ceased suddenly as though the car had toppled into the sea. I stumbled towards the road, in alarm, but that voice still rose down the soft, sandy road to the quay. The mystery of the wreck would remain unsolved. The captain had come back at last for his men.

IV

In the morning sunlight, I passed down the one street, broad and quiet, of the little town. The saddler looked through his dusty window pane, a piece of blackened twine between his lips, and a few old fellows nodded at me from a corner. The flock of geese which was congregated at the cobbled market place as usual moved

132

ceremoniously as though heavy with solemn memories. Always I regarded them with awe for they reminded me of the sacred seven at the Capitol and I swear often in memory at the lively young ganger watching the far hills for the smoke sign which tells that treacle is on the boil in an illicit still. He assured me that those great birds disappeared promptly at the Christmas festival. Beyond the street, I saw the sandhills, yellow in the sunlight as cornfields. When the rain and mist sweep in from the Atlantic, these dunes seem to ooze a pale light.

As I crossed the long bridge over the strait, I looked down at the blue pools and streaks left by the tide. On the Island, as the big headland is called, I stopped at a little crossroads. A girl came swinging past the bend and sand as if she had come from the sky. I asked her the way.

'That road on the right,' she said, pointing, 'will bring you to the front of the Island, and that one on the left will bring you to the back side.'

Blushing, I murmured hasty thanks and turned right. For many hours I wandered down boreens and clefts that brought me to rock and foam, went past hens, ducks, to half-doors, where women, shouting at dogs, told me that they could not put me up. So I was hurried from cottage to cottage until all the evasive words took shape and came to this: That one James So-and-so had a fine house all to himself. He was absent indeed. Where was he? At the Fair of Creoshla, but he would be back with the night.

I set off with my manuscript book under my arm towards the horn of the cape, crossed a bogland, came to a green height so fine that the four winds might come to dance there. I ate my sandwiches, whittled away the hours watching the waters far below until the sun had turned behind the jags of the sea-mountains and flamed across the waves. I guessed that the fair was over, the drink and the horses gone home.

I turned back and came at last to the small, well-built house of James So-and-so. A man was standing smoking outside the next door. 'Is he in?' I asked. The man took the clay pipe from his lips, looked into the west and after a long while, replied, 'He's in the States'. 'You're a liar, he's at the Fair of Creoshla.' I turned away angrily.

I had heard that an Englishwoman was living with a ghost in the last cottage on the cape. I would ask the foreigner for a night's shelter, brave her clammy lodger. It was twilight when I came towards the cottage. On the nearby slope, I met the woman carrying a basket of white washing. She brought me in, hurried from dresser to fire and table, making a fine meal for me, while I talked to the woman's guest from Birmingham who was staying with her. There was no room in the house. Would I mind sleeping in the loft? Gladly, I carried out rugs into the dark, while the kettle was boiling. My hostess held a storm lantern while I climbed beyond the half-awake hens into the warmth of hay, good for rest, sweet-smelling as apples. After supper, as I sat at the fire, listening to the dull sound of the surge below the cliffs, my hostess told me about the ghost; she did not mind it: at any moment it might rattle milk-pans in the little dairy, rap on the wall. Suddenly there was a loud knocking. 'The ghost!' I exclaimed, jumping up. The Englishwoman looked troubled and went to the door. I heard the murmur of a man's voice outside.

'That was the landlord,' she said, coming back. 'He won't allow anyone to stay here.'

'Not even in the loft?'

'No, what are we to do?'

She had to live there, so I decided to go. The sea was louder below the cliffs.

'Does he live far from here?'

'Over a mile, by the back road.'

I said goodbye to her and the friend.

At a quick pace, I set out to find the landlord, angry words filling my mind. The moon was in the south-east as I crossed the fallow, leaped over the gleam of the bog-drains. Cottages were clustered below in a dark hollow. An old man hobbled up towards me. The moon glittered on his reverend beard.

Where does So-and-so live?'

'I never heard of him,' he said slowly and toiled past me.

A young fellow came, swinging lightly as a colt, out of the night. Fixing him with an eye, I led him on as my unwilling guide. Suddenly, from the hollow the shrill voice of a woman rushed after us, 'Johnnie, Johnnie', it screamed, and the youth, tearing himself from the trance, took to his heels.

While I stood wondering, I became aware of forms gathering

from the darkness. I heard an angry murmur. All seemed unreal, something I had read. In alarm, I waited. There was nothing to do but face the onset. A gust of whisky came nearer. Violent faces were thrust in mine.

'You've no right here,' shouted a big planter.

'As much as you,' I said, backing from him.

Their movements were threatening. I must try to bluff them. So I took all into my confidence with extreme cordiality. I was astray ... the road dark ... the day had been fine ... the crops looked good ... the turf firm ... did they use a loy here ... had the Fair been a big one?

I felt their sudden bewilderment, the ground was changed. Their minds were bending down to find their bit of quarrel again. At last the big man said more quietly: 'Well, we'll see you off the Island'.

So with two men abreast and a dozen tramping after us, I was marched down the road, palavering, gabbling about corn, fishing, rye, grass, cattle, sheep-dip, turf, concealing my ignorance of farming in a rush of words, oblivious of moon and road, aware of the silent marchers behind me. We seemed to have been tramping for an hour, though we had gone little more than a mile. There was a mumble, a shuffle of turning hobnails. I was alone.

In the south, beyond a bank of mist was the top of Muckish. In the silence, I heard spring water near me. Peewits were crying in the distance, as I left the Island.

A few days later, I decided to go out to Tory Island. Although all told me that I would not be allowed to live there, I would not believe it. So I got on my bicycle and soon was speeding along the sea-road, past the Gaelic College at Falcaragh, through Gortahork, watching the distant peak of Errigal, wondering whether Deirdre and the Sons of Usnach had fled through the north-west glens from the rage of the King of Ulster. I turned west to Bloody Foreland: all was desolate, bogland, tidal reefs. When I had gone about ten miles, I swerved around a corner and saw the Ballad-man.

Eighteen

I

IT WAS AT THE TURN OF THE ROAD that I saw him first, his back against the low seawall as the sun was going down into the ocean. Outside the little public house, a knot of islanders, urged by the shrill voice of a woman, was jeering him. One low-sized, dark-skinned fellow with a red kerchief twisted round his neck, capered about him, grimacing, with a jack-knife. The ballad-man, hunched in his rags, was crying, and though his tears were stock-in-trade, they seemed real, terrible, mixing with laughter where nothing was near but heatherlands with chill pools of light and, beyond them, the plains of the running tide. His whining seemed inhuman, the seal's cry, the cry of the fool driven by rain and mockery, poor Tom, for all his guile, a-cold. Unable to stand it, I crossed his hand with a sixpenny piece. He stared at it, bit it, stared again until his eyes seemed to blaze silver. Like that of a child, his whim changed and he leaped up merrily. The crowd changed with him. They watched with eagerness the old ritual of song. First he picked up a few pebbles carefully, as though assaying them, knotted them into a coloured rag, then he put a few stones crossways on the road as though with a last memory of the sword-dance, and seriously, as when children play hop-scotch.

He droned a Gaelic song and at each end of the tune he took a run, leap, and a couple of hurrying steps, whirling the weighted kerchief in a little fury around his head. I can only remember a few words about red apples on a branch, that in the salt air, filled my mind with a rich taste. I cut him a quid of black twisted tobacco. The islanders beat their hands.

He danced again. He sang again. I cannot remember what the words were, yet they were about a man who had been angered by a woman, and as I stood among the sallow island folk of some other race, I wondered who had made this song which had tumbled down

to rags, known this bitterness, which a bit of silver and a cut of
tobacco had called back out of a century. Had I not my own share
of trouble, seeing that a face had driven my feet to the west, and my
own complaints?

> Though I had caught the knowledgeable salmon
> Out of the unlighted waters at Cong,
> Fasted off holy islands where the sail
> Still bends a knee, I had not thought, O Woman
> With the dark hair, that you would make the priest
> Talk from the altar and our love as common
> As holy water at the chapel door.

I thought of the ranns and ballad dancers of Rome and of the
learned Goliards drinking, swearing, story-telling, in refectory and
tavern, before the green of Spring had come, of MacConglinne who
had cured a possessed king by the devilment of his own songs, of
the Mongaire Sugach, musical as a thrush, who had been driven
from every parish, of Blind Raftery, the last of them, singing of a
woman, the star of knowledge, whom he could not see, and how
that poetry had gone into books when mouth and heel had grown
strange to one another. But already the ballad-maker was tramping
down the road, no doubt to the other public house I had passed on
the way. I praise, now, his tact and patience.

I went in. A tall old man caught me by the tie as I passed. I had
noticed him before out of the corner of my eye, leaning, bearded,
above the balladry, with extraordinary disgust. I knew from his eye
and the largeness of his slouch hat that he had known wide spaces
of island and ocean. I remembered the City of the Tribes: old
merchants that had bargained in Spain: lace, wine and sweet-wood
kegs, dark sails, now, and nets and brown shiny ribbon from the
rocks: these people, these things, I saw.

'You're not one of them,' said the old man, jerking his shoulder
towards the swarthy islanders who were jabbering excitedly in
Gaelic above their tumblers.

'You're a Mayo man like myself.'

'I am not then.'

'You've a hat like me, and God's truth, a bow like myself,' he
replied. 'You're a Mayo man.'

137

We left it at that and, in drink, in silence, I was of his clan.

A red-haired woman looked in at the door.

He leaned over and roared into my ear: 'O Mother o' God, it's a wicked world. What do you think I saw last night in a byre as I was going home? A man and a cow. . . .'

A crowd of men got between us. When we were jostled together again, he was talking dreamily of something else.

'I was coming home one day, and it got dark all of a sudden, and there was I straying about for hours in a field praying to the Holy Mother with the sweat pouring off me in bucketfuls, and it suddenly came into my mind to turn my coat inside out, and when I'd done that, there I was on the road again in the middle of the day.'

'Now that's all God's truth,' he added as I called for more porter. 'And I wouldn't tell it to you only you've seen Them yourself and you a Mayo man like me. But there was one of them Yankees here once, going around looking for information about Them, he was. The boys had rare sport, cracking with that fellow-me-lad, and filling his head, and they say he put it all down in a big book over in the States.'

I had read that book on *Celtic Fairylore,* but I did not let him know that I had. The comments of the folk on the enthusiasts who had gone down among them with sharp pencil and gaping mouth would redden many an ear that I respect. The old man went on from drink to drink. He told me of the store of music that lies hid in the grass of Ballymore – but those who will may find it for themselves, and if they put foot on the hunger-grass, they will have such music as makes wit and heart wander, and he told me of cattle driven under enchantment through the night from a rath seven miles away and of fishing boats that were sunk by an old woman who puts bits of wood in their likeness into a tub of water, angry with spells, and in a hoarser voice he hinted again of the unspeakable things that are forbidden in the Books of Deuteronomy.

It was near to dark and I could hear the islanders shouting and cursing from the shore, the lessening creak of the row-locks.

The old man suddenly got up, steadied himself, looked at me darkly as though he had never seen me before, and went out.

'Did you know who that oul' fella was?' asked the barman, winking.

I did not, but I winked back.

It was twilight when I got outside. A cold light blew from the westward ocean and the far cries of boatmen. So alone, on the edge of night, I walked, remembering the treachery of a woman.

II

At sunset, I sat in the public-house conspiring as to how I might visit the Island. I had been told that it was hardly possible, for the simple folk that lived there were shy of strangers. It was a wild ultimate place; in fact I was in the last public house in the world. Beyond lay the ocean, still gleaming, and the dry parish of America. A group of islanders, dark-haired men, of some race that was not Irish, were drinking there. I began by talking to the youngest of them and the merriest. There is no liquor on the Island. Years ago the King of the Island had a thriving trade. A mission or 'station' was held there and the evils of drink were denounced. The King, with a magnificent gesture, put the shutters up – incidentally having made his money. As a result, the islanders, who are a logical people, come over to the mainland when the fishing has been good and get glorious until the money runs out. They do not burn kelp since it went down to three pounds a ton, for they are proud, also.

This young man was returning to the Island after a fortnight in Ireland. The other men gathered around us and I called for drinks. Much to the surprise of my pocket, they ordered whiskies. Having got them, they went back to their corner and began to talk earnestly. Small as my share of Irish was, I heard the word 'punta' repeated very often with figures that made me uneasy and seeing that they glanced over at me as they spoke, I guessed what they were saying. The merry young man whispered to me in broken English that they were considering what I was worth for the voyage. He told me of the postman who was going over in the morning, a reasonable agent, and we slipped out to find him.

It was darkfall outside. Far beyond, I saw the tower-like cliffs of Tory, where the sea-gods, the pirate Fomors, were once fortressed. Below, we heard the shouts of islanders as they pushed their boats into the sea. We passed the hill-cottages and before us, Bloody Foreland loomed in the last light. My companion insisted that we must climb the cape, but as it was more than nine hundred feet high and separated from us by dangerous bogland, I dragged him away. We whistled and the postman came out of the night.

The morning was clear. I stood beside the sea watching a man cutting turf against the sky-line and felt, toned by distance, the dignity of laborious movement. I made my way by gorse and rapped on the half-door of a cottage to ask for a drink of water, as I was thirsty from smoking. To my surprise, the woman there gave me a bowl of sweet milk.

The men had come down by the cliff path. We pushed the hooker down the rollers and soon the sail was lifted. Halfway out, the wind dropped and the men rowed on one side of the boat, while I played treasonable music on a mouth-organ, or as it is called here, a 'French fiddle'. On our right spread many capes and the blue slopes of the Donegal mountains.

As I played, I thought of a warning story I had heard. The islanders once woke up a doctor on the mainland. Someone was ill on Tory. The night was cold and wild. The doctor asked for an impossible sovereign. To his sorrow, they put their heads together and produced the piece of gold. Having come with them and seen the case, which was not serious, he thought about getting home. The islanders were peacefully smoking on the quay or mending their nets. He suggested the desirability of returning to Ireland. They were surprised but said, 'We'll take you back for two sovereigns'.

When I was safely on the little pier, I told the postman that I would pay him when I got back to the mainland. He and all the crew assured me that no stranger would be lodged on the Island and so I would have to return with them. I shook my head and waited until they had loaded the hooker with barrels of fish and set sail again. Having metaphorically burned my boat behind me, I set out to see the King.

He was an agreeable old man. We talked about modern Gaelic writings for a long while. He was sorry indeed that he could not put me up in his house. I left him and went into a cottage and asked for food. The woman could not give me a bed for she had ten sons in the house, but she put milk and large hunks of potato cake before me. I was aware of what seemed multitudes of men passing in and out of the house, yet when I began to eat, I noticed a strange silence in the sunlit kitchen. It was deserted. I blessed their delicate consideration and, having eaten, I sat down on a form near the smouldering turf-fire and made with pent-up feelings a traditional curse on the King:

Black luck upon you, Seamus Mac-an-Bhaird,
Who shut the door upon a poet
Nor put red wine and bread upon the board;
My song is greater than your hoard,
Although running children know it
Between the sea and the windy stones.

Yet, Seamus of the Bards, when you are dead
And the curragh carries out the new coffin,
Heavy with you within, heavy with lead . . .

'Inisbofin', 'unfed', 'windy stones' with its echo of 'bones', the rhymes made the curse grimmer than I had meant it to be.

I wandered through the village, half-tumbled beneath the ruined round tower of Columcille, but no one would take me in. It was turning late and the thought of having to stretch in one of the seal-caves was not consoling. I noticed that all the folk agreed that the lighthouse was the place for me, large, comfortable, tons of room. I set out towards the point of the island. I saw with pleasure the large empty buildings around the light-tower. Certainly a whole school of Irish poets could be lodged in them. I had not reckoned with the conscience of the keeper of the light.

'I couldn't, sir. What if the Head Commissioner of Lights came down from Dublin and found a stranger on the premises?'

'Good God, man,' I cried, growing angry with the increasing darkness, 'do you think the head buck cat is going to come down from Dublin in the middle of the night?'

His integrity was not to be shaken. His assistant followed me out and told me how sorry he was that he could do nothing for me. We sat on the sea-rocks and as I watched the silver band of light narrowing in the west and felt already the desolation of the night, he told of his experiences in a Kerry lighthouse. A few years previously, when he was still there, he had seen Roger Casement landing from a German submarine. For an hour, the stories went on. One of them he had heard from the islanders.

'There was a man here in the lighthouse and he made free with

141

a girl and left the island. Nobody knew and when her time was come, she went down to the caves where the seals do be, and was never found again. Fifteen years afterwards, a man came with a gun to shoot seals. He fired at what he thought was a seal and heard the scream of a young girl and then. . . .'

The mention of seal-caves brought me back to reality and shivering with the chill of night, I left him in the middle of his story. As I walked back the mile in darkness to the village, I met an old man. His one joy was to read books in Gaelic during the winter. I promised him more than his head could hold in a season. He warmed towards me and brought me in to one of his neighbours.

Once the strangeness was broken, they were a kindly, generous people. I was put before the warm turf and a large steamy bowl of 'stirabout' was filled for me from the pot on the hook. I grew sleepy but before I reached that last contentment, I was to be surprised once more.

III

'There are no rats at all on the Island,' said the man of the house, suddenly, as I nodded by the fire. The neighbours had come in to see the stranger and they sat around on the settles. 'There was a saint here long ago,' said one of them, 'and she was buried near the old tower. Her two brothers were saints also, but when they were dead and buried, the graves were found open at dawn. That happened many times until the people took thought to bury them with their sister. They found rest after that. The clay from their graves drives out rats. There is only one family around here can lift the clay, and the hole in the grave is never any bigger.'

On the day I left, I found that the family I had stayed with were the hereditary guardians of the grave, but all had been too shy to tell me. They gave me a little bag of the clay and said that it could only be used with belief and prayer. 'Tá colaidh orm anois,' I said, and one of the brothers lit a candle with a sod and left me in the room where I was to sleep. There were two old-fashioned featherbeds with canopies over them and side-curtains, placed end to end. I tumbled out of my clothes and into the nearest one. In a little while, I heard scampering noises over my head. I thought that if it were mice up there, they were unusually large, no doubt, to make up for the absence of rats. As I sank towards sleep, dreaming that scores of large mice were plumping towards my face, I heard strange wheezing sounds.

'Who is that?' I cried in Irish.

A voice that seemed full of the centuries came from the curtain beyond my toes. Much relieved, I gathered that it was an old man that was in the other bed. We talked of winter storm, of tobacco and drink, until we drowsed off. When I woke up in the morning he was gone. We talked every night through the dull red curtains, but I never saw him and he remained an aged coughing voice. I looked from the little window that morning at the ridges and peaks of Ireland, the light crossing over with the tide.

The women moved about the house and shore barefoot. The men sat smoking on the door-stone, talking with me of the clouds bearing from the foreland – a sign that the day was fairing – and of the gannets that pass the Island and do not rest until they come to Fanet Head. A few men were out in curraghs on the brighter water, using a paddle as if they were digging for sea-potatoes with a spade. There was a large patchwork quilt stretched out to air in the sun: it was a craze of dazzling colours against rock and ocean.

The Island is full of horses and the dark-haired girls gallop on them fearlessly without saddle or bit, carrying big creels of sods. There are patches of oats and barley, of an intense rich green as though the barren strength of the island had gathered into those few spots. All around, the surface had been picked bare, for the knotted sods are burned with the turf that is brought over by oar and sail from Magheroarty – the plain of the spring-tide.

The northward side of the island ends in the great legendary cliffs of Balor against which the winter storms break. On my way there, I came to a little bay under the Tor where a princess had been imprisoned long ago. As I swam in the green waters, men gathered on the headland and with angry gestures called down that I was a stranger and had no right to be there. I recognized them as the swarthy men I had met in the public house and to whom I gave the slip. After we had flung bits of hard words above and below, they went off towards the eastern village.

I set out for the Cursing Stone. This is a great boulder, balanced on the edge of a precipice about seven hundred feet above the sea, half in, half out. In the old days, Lord Leitrim sent out a gun-boat, *The Wasp*, to collect rents that had never been paid, but an old woman went up to the stone and turned it leftways against the enemy and the sun. The warship sank in the calm waters in sight of the anxious islanders. That was the last attempt to exact tribute: the islanders rule themselves and their laws, mainly about fishing, are intricate. The tide brought the drowned crew back to Ireland and their wide grave may be seen in the little Protestant churchyard at Killult. Later I stayed for a month within a stone's throw of the tomb, in a little cottage where Aodh de Blacam, the novelist, lived. On nights, a few men who were writing plays and novels in Irish struck in. But that small cultural movement was stopped and all were held in the prisons taken over by their former friends. So for a time, it seemed that a price had been put upon the very head of literature.

The Stone, when rightly used, is also a Wishing Rock. I stood there swaying the stone and wished, in that sudden moment of dangerous dizziness that such a precipice brings, for the woman I was in love with for several years. And though it seemed unlikely then, I got my wish, but that Stone, like all oracles, was ambiguous and turned my thoughts for so long against the sun that even that barren island seemed desirable to me.

> Were I in Clare of the ships,
> Drinking with fishermen, I would not care,
> Not I, not I, until the keg ran dry.
> Or were I sailing on a windy morrow
> By Tory, where the barefoot women work,
> And a man can take a bellyful of ease
> Nor fear the rats of sorrow.
> > Were I backward
> At a lake, when reeds were slipping their young shadows
> Like black eels, I would take no care, not I,
> Not I.

Far below, thousands of seagulls circled with a wild music like the skirling of innumerable bagpipes. A sea-puffin sat within arm's reach of me, totally indifferent.

He had a black frockcoat and cravat, a white waistcoat, a red curved nose, suggestive of dissipation, and tawny spats. The

Torymen call the puffins 'Protestants'. The man who told me said that the black-and-white oyster-catcher, so delicate in its flight, was known as the 'Catholic', but I knew by his eye that he was making it up. While I lay on the brink of the cliff, a tall fellow loitered up from the slope. I knew in the distance that he was queer and grasped my stick. But he was only an amadaun. When I took out the old silver watch that the Man of the House had lent me, he implored me to give it to him and wept like a child. When I put it back quickly, he stammered.

'Then give me money.' 'How much?' I asked curiously.

'Half a crown,' said the fool. So I gave him a shilling for his wits. He ran down towards the stricken east village. Few of the people would say anything to me of that place and from a safe distance I fancied that the figures I saw there moved about in an odd way. Inbreeding and salt fish may have had their way.

There is a proverb that those who say they will go to Tory, even though jestingly, must find themselves there alive or dead. Though it was once a funeral island, dancing is in it every night and the sound of the fiddle near the waters. As one looks from the coast at the tors, dark against the sunset, they seem full of strange significance, so I had seen them at darkfall and thought of the Turning of the Stone.

> The red Armada of the sun burned down
> From Magheroarty: melodeons played
> *The Waves of Tory* and the young girls sat
> Upon the knees of men. I took my sup,
> I kissed the mouth beside me and forgot
> My sorrow and the cold dark tide.

IV

After I came back from Tory, I stayed in a public house in the glen beneath Errigal. As I was wandering by the riverside about four o'clock, I came at a sandy bend on two wild-looking girls beetling clothes. One of them was ugly and squat, her red flannel petticoat tucked into a monstrous lump round her buttocks and, as she pounded and stamped upon the sinking clothes, her legs, splotched with chill water, were purplish as ling. The other was tall, a lazybones with a golden head, wringing out beads from a pillow case. I saw her as in a dream. The contrast was so much that of a fairy tale that I went back to far-off times, thinking of a King's house in the mountains, and of women dipping the webs into vats full of sea-scarlet and of the shuttle jumping to laughter. As if in answer to my epic thought, the ugly one caught sight of me.

'Arra, a man,' she shrieked, bursting into mirth, kicking and pounding the waters with sudden frenzy. Both of them seemed to dance in the waters now – laughing, rocking, lashing it to foam.

'He's shy,' exclaimed the ugly one, twisting with merriment.

'You're not one of them Papishers?' said the slender girl, tossing her bright head like a filly. 'I don't like them.'

I was suddenly back in the Christian era. But the other danced in the middle of the stream, rocking with laughter to a sort of mad tune.

'Meet us tonight, tonight, at the House, then, then, it's full of hay, full of hay!'

A few sheep looked inquisitively over the ridge, and in a moment a wild young man was amongst us.

He had a large bottle of milkish liquor. He talked, swore, tricked, as he gulped the raw whisky. We quarrelled over the lanky girl. Suddenly he disappeared, as he had come, over the hill. A minute after I saw him charging down the bank towards me, waving the empty bottle. The girls worked in the water silently, as though they had but one eye between them. The most unaccustomed mind moves in a flash in such a case; two things leaped to mine – the glinting rifles that I had seen as I crossed the hills the night before and a picture in a book that I had read when a boy with the words underneath: 'If you move another inch, Mr. Mann, I'll blow your brains out'.

I put my hands to my empty hip pocket, repeated the words with a violent adjective or two. The trick worked. The young man took to his heels so comically that I laughed, thinking to have seen the last of him; but we were destined to meet once more when the moon came from behind Errigal.

There was a dance in the glen that night. The cottage was full of people. Around the room the girls sat on the knees of men. Many feet jigged on the stoney flags of the kitchen while the concertina went in and out.

There was another ballad-singer there that night, evidently of higher rank, for he was sitting next to the turf fire. He was an old man with long white hair. By day he walked the roads, they said, and at sunset came upon fire and merriment.

Because of the stranger, he chanted a long ballad in English about Napoleon: for the tradition of that small man still lingers out a century in these mountain places. The boys and girls listened with respect, though their feet were restless enough, but when he had come to what must have been the fiftieth verse, somebody sent round a cap and pennies crowded eagerly into it.

He danced, then, a jig, barefooted and whistling; and the man of the house, as old and white, clapped and clawed him with delight. So once more the concertina went in and out merrily and the dancers crossed in a reel.

On the roads after the dance, I met a few lads making for the hayloft near the House, to have some sport, as they said, and remembering my tryst with the bright-headed woman, I went with them. As we drew towards a gate barred in shadows, the soft laughter of hidden girls beckoned us on.

Suddenly a dog leaped out of the night. It seemed to me as gigantic, as loud as the hound that had guarded the forge of the demon-smith, Cullan, in the far mountains, and with the others, I tore down the boreen. Dark figures followed the hound, brandishing what looked like spears, but were, as my shoulder learned, merely broomsticks.

In a moment we were all mixed up in fight and stick rang abruptly upon stick. In the moonlight, I saw the tousled head of the young man who had threatened me with the bottle. For what seemed an hour, we lashed wildly at each other, and ash parried broom. Suddenly the struggle melted away, curses and cries thinned; the attackers had disappeared as rapidly as they had come.

My companions were gone. Silence flowed in round my head. I saw Errigal and far below the two lakes glittering in the moon, as, black of heart, I walked the road to my bed, meditating upon the treachery of women.

Nineteen

GRADUALLY, as we drank during the afternoon and our senses were doubling, Father Macadoo seemed to change in the middle of the tobacco smoke and I saw before me the merry round figure of Old Father William emerge from Lewis Carroll's poem. With a fatuous grin, he bounced from one of the enormous armchairs in the drawing-room of the presbytery, seemed to spin like a tee-totum in the air, and then descend into the equally enormous armchair on the opposite side of the hearth-rug. Outside, in the September sunlight, the village was as silent as its parish church and the geese near the weigh-house were somnolent. When I visited him for the first time, Father Macadoo was troubled by an unusual problem. I refused the double whisky which he offered me and he was cast down. Then, in an instant, with an eager smile, he recovered and endeavoured to convert me.

'You should always drink whisky, my child. It was ordained by God Himself to counteract the bad effects of our damp climate. He paused as he reached for the bottle of ten-year old. 'You should always drink whisky,' he lilted, as he drained joyfully his own glass and poured himself another drink.

Suddenly there was a discreet knock at the door.

Winking at me, he hid the bottle and the two glasses in the sideboard. Then he drew himself up, with the grave appearance of a wise old parish priest: 'Come in,' he called.

His housekeeper, who was of the correct canonical age, appeared.

'There's a woman here to see you Father.'

'I won't be a second,' he said to me.

In a short while he was back again, but the problem of what I should drink was still worrying him. At last, his face brightened and he waddled into the next room. He was back again, almost before the clock on the mantelpiece could tick, bearing a bottle with great care.

'This is an excellent wine,' he explained. 'It was recommended to me years ago by a Jesuit and I always use it at Mass. As you know, they always choose the best.'

So with the feeling that I was committing a minor sacrilege, I drank that delicious wine and soon with a foolish smile I was watching Father Macadoo as he bounded from his armchair and revolved like a lit Catherine Wheel, and then descended accurately on the other armchair which took with its expensive upholstery and springs that ample shock without a sound. As he became tipsier, he grew serious, drew me paternally towards the window and, gazing at the western sky with his hand on my shoulder spoke to me soulfully of the strange destiny of our country.

Several years later, I realized that he had drawn his admirable sentiments from *John Bull's Other Island*.

John Masefield, G. K. Chesterton, Douglas Goldring and other English writers, lured by the conversation of A.E., had visited that north-west corner of County Donegal in summer time. Father Macadoo assured me that all of them had been impressed by his discourse on the spiritual mission of Inisfail.

With much pride, on our second afternoon together, he brought me into the next room. The walls were lined with mahogany shelves and he showed me on them, much to my surprise, a remarkable collection of books about Napoleon. I was free, he said, to borrow as many of those volumes as I wished. Enthusiastically and at length, he spoke of his hero and every time I came back to drink the sacramental wine, we discussed the books which he had lent to me. One afternoon, with a run of chuckles, he confided to me:

'This morning, as I was saying Mass, a new idea about the Battle of Lodi came to me right in the very middle of what I was saying.'

He chuckled again as he explained his theory. So, for a month, I read in a daze as many of those volumes about Napoleon as I could, and came back to discuss them.

One afternoon, Father Macadoo took a framed photograph of a clerical student from the sideboard and handed it to me.

'Does that remind you of anyone?'

He watched me anxiously, almost pleadingly, and I knew that I must not disappoint him. Suddenly inspiration came to me.

149

'It reminds me of the young Bonaparte.'

Delighted by my perspicacity, he admitted shyly that it was a photograph of himself in his first year at Maynooth. We pledged that notable resemblance in whisky and altar wine.

Sometimes in indignation, Father Macadoo inveighed against his wicked uncle, the aged Bishop of the diocese, because that turbulent ecclesiastic had steadily refused to promote his convivial nephew.

'I forgive him,' exclaimed Father Macadoo, 'for all he has done against me. And I have my consolation.'

He gazed wistfully from the window at the sunset and repeated those mystical sentiments which he had borrowed so often from Shaw.

I have but to close my eyes now to see once more that good friend of mine – whose advice I had failed to take – bounce in the middle of a sentence from his enormous armchair, spin like a top, and then descend, safe and sound, into the equally enormous armchair at the other side of the hearth-rug.

II

One evening, Father Macadoo suggested that I should accompany a young priest who was visiting relatives near Falcarragh, for this would give me an opportunity of seeing more of Donegal. So, on the following morning, I drove off from the Presbytery in a hired Ford car with Father McElligott, a tall man of about thirty years of age. He had spent several years on the English Mission, that dream which has lingered in Ireland since the Jacobite struggle of the seventeenth century – that dream of a Catholic monarch on the throne and the restoral of obedience to the Papacy. Many an Irish priest lives out that illusion in an industrial town of Lancashire or in a remote village of Wales, saying Mass at morning in back-room or mission-shed with a dozen old women as his congregation.

The driver turned southward and we passed on our right the ridge of sandhills near Horn Head. Far away across the waters of the Atlantic, which were calm as the low sky that morning, we could see the rain-coloured cliffs of Tory Island. Beyond bogland was the tilted brink of Muckish, which Shane Leslie has described in a fine lyric:

Muckish, greatest pig in Ulster's oak-woods,
Littered out of rock and fire,
Deep you thrust your mottled flanks for cooling
Underneath the peaty mire.

Muckish, you will not forget the people
Of the laughing speech and eye,
They who gave you name of Pig-back-mountain
And the Heavens for a sty!

We sped past many a hill-road along which I would have liked to stray, for I could see, here and there, the last tops of the fox glove and purple patches of loosestrife. Everywhere were farmlets with field walls of loose stone, greener after-grass, tilled plots between the boulders. Soon, we saw, mist-drawn in the distance, the peak of Errigal, the thick-set cloud-shadows between the Acla Mountains. Beyond them, along the coast with its scattered miles of showers, were all those creeks and tumbling streams of the Glenties which I had never seen.

Almost all Irish priests are sons of well-to-do publicans, shop-keepers or 'gombeen men' and when we reached Falcarragh, my companion began his round of visits to counter and parlour. Everywhere His Reverence was greeted with the traditional hundred thousand welcomes. Everywhere His health was drunk in the best Irish whisky. I had to share in that hospitality, while around us a chorus of shopkeepers, wives, gathering friends, kept repeating: 'Oh Father! Yes, Father. Do you say so, Father!'

After a substantial meal, we drove on to the townland of Gortahork, stopping here and there for another round of drinks. At last the car was shoving itself up muddy boreens, bathing, grinding in low gear, for Father McElligott, inspired by his copious potations, had insisted on visiting the hillside cottagers whom he had known as a lad. Ganders hissed, hens fled with homeward squawks, donkeys galloped beyond the thorn trees, dogs barked at us. Half-doors opened. We stooped, stumbled into kitchens, sat down by the turf-fire, while the Man of the House and his wife greeted us, their children astare with wondering eyes. In and out we went, emptying tumblers, while the chorus spread from the east to the west of the little houses.

'Oh Father! Yes, Father. Do you say so, Father?'

At darkfall, we were on our return journey and by this time Father McElligott was stotious. At the last house to which we called, he was asked to give a young married woman a lift and the three of us got into the back of the car. We had scarcely gone a mile when Father McElligott yielded to sudden temptation. He made wild attempts to hug the comely wife and fondle the plump pair of breasts under her blouse. Embarrassed, yet respectful, she tried to push away the holy Father, who almost fell on top of her every time the car swayed on the rough road. 'Oh Father! No, Father!' she exclaimed at each encounter. In virtuous indignation – though I was almost as much tempted as His Reverence – I endeavoured to keep him away from her, but the task was a difficult one and so it was a relief when we arrived at last at the Presbytery. I helped the missioner to get out of the car, and we said goodbye to the young woman as the driver started off again.

On the door-step, Father Macadoo was waiting for us anxiously, and I suspect that he glanced at us with contempt as, arm in arm, we staggered along the gravel path.

Twenty

ONE SUNDAY EVENING, I cycled with our large landlady to a farm, a few miles away, where she was accustomed to buy new-laid eggs. I met there a tall, dark-haired girl of twenty-one, who had come over from a neighbouring farm. When the gossip became closer after tea, my landlady suggested that Elspeth should take me out and show me the view. Later I was to wonder whether that fortune-teller had brought together by design the tea-leaves in our two teacups.

We strolled a few hundred yards and sat on a stone wall, looking across the wild tract of heather and ruck, towards Sheephaven. I lit a cigarette for Elspeth, and expertly, she blew smoke rings into the air, her fine legs crossed. Suddenly she began to laugh – and when I asked her the reason she told me a story about a commercial traveller who was alone with a girl in a railway carriage. He was reading a magazine called *The Jumper* and she misunderstood his intentions, when he leaned over and said politely, 'Would you care to see it?' Despite my shyness, I took the broad hint and asked her when we could meet again. Unforbidden Fruit got down from the wall, took my hand, and brought me to the brink of the hill. She pointed to a small wood at the far end of the Ards, a long ridge towards the south. She told me to go up the path to the wood and wait there the next night at about eight o'clock. I would find a ring of bracken surrounded by small trees. She would come there as soon as she had given her father and brother their supper.

On Monday evening, I went up the rocky path between trees to the top. I could see some miles away the strand at Marble Hill and the edges of the foam, pale-flowering, and opposite, the dark drop of Muckish. I turned and found in a few moments the secret circle of bracken, entirely surrounded by larch and by rowan with bunches of crimson berries. In the dusk, the bracken had a metallic gleam and I hesitated before I waded, waist-deep, through it. But the bracken sprang back again and I sank down under fronds, hidden from all except the sky. I leaned on an elbow, smoking my pipe in that pleasant place where the air was too cool for midgets. Darkness came and soon I could hear Elspeth rustling through the bracken, see her face gleam in the moonlight. A few minutes later, we lay in each other's arms, our mouths pressed closely together before our hands began discovering those Protestant and Catholic differences which have troubled so many throughout the centuries. I call her the Protestant girl, though strictly speaking, she was a Presbyterian. The Border soon disappeared: North and South were one.

Every evening we met in that circle of moonlight and shadow. Often Elspeth laughed, insisting that I was enjoying her wrongly. I recalled how St. Alphonso de Liguouri and other theologians had discussed this matter in their Latin Treatises – *situs innaturalis est si coitus fiat praepostere more pecudem*. No doubt, it was the traditional custom in that remote townland at the back of Godspeed. Sometimes, to reassure my darling, I played Jove to her Europa, but she was so reckless with all that was under her skirt that I had to exercise much restraint, behaving like so many young husbands who have hoped recently that the Ecumenical Council would have pity on their plight. Yet some medieval casuists averred that withdrawal is a venial offence, although it leads to over-indulgence. Others maintained the contrary:

> Per verbum 'cohaere' intelligitur cohaerentia usque ad perfectam capulum, seu seminationem perfectum, ita ut per se mortal sit, inchoatam, capulam abrumpere.

I did not trouble Elspeth with these learned conjectures, as we fondled each other under the fronds.

Long after midnight, we stole quietly hand in hand down the path between the trees.

Sometimes, in the afternoon, I made my way down the boreens to the white-washed cottage where Elspeth lived. She greeted me at the half-door and brought me into the cottage. She was always in her Sunday skirt and wore a gay jumper, light purple in colour, which she had knitted herself. Clearly it showed the nipples of her breasts. She sat down, crossing her shapely legs, proud of her white rayon stockings, as she puffed a cigarette. We talked, kissed and parted, knowing that we would meet again in a few hours.

At dark, I climbed the ridge of Ards and stole under the rowan branches, heavy with berries. Hidden in the bracken, I rested on an elbow, smoking my pipe until I heard, faint with longing, a rustle coming towards me. I reached up my arms and drew down Elspeth from the moon. Long after midnight, we stole down the path among the trees, carefully avoiding the trip and twist of roots. A watchdog on one of the small farms below was sure to bark: that challenge in the stillness of the night would be answered by yelping from a neighbouring farm and then from the next half-a-dozen holdings. Often I fancied that the barking spread along the coast by Falcarragh, Gortahork, beyond Errigal and the Poisoned Glen, the inlets of the Rosses and the Glenties, until it multiplied itself throughout the length and breadth of Ireland, so that Bishops, parish priests, curates, stirred uneasily in their slumber, dreaming of the sins committed by young couples at night in barns, haylofts or behind the hedges of the Central Plain.

Twenty One

DESPITE THE DANGER OF CIVIL WAR between the forces of the new Provisional Government and the Republicans, I decided to venture on the long train journey to Killarney. As we came towards Kerry, I thought on an unusual poem by James Cousins, *The Fire of Love, the Wine of Love and the Wings*:

> For my eyes, half closed, will have slid from the
>   mountain's head
> To the woody side where the earliest flame of the sunlight
>   broke
> On the soft young larches whose heads go up in smoke.

I could see in my mind the Lower Lake:

> I will walk by the shore of Loch Lein when the midday spell
> Lies flat on the looking-glass where the purple peak
> Stands still on its head, like a clown at a fair; and the cackle
>   and shriek
> Of the blackbird in nesting-time is echoed from elm and ash.

I was the only stranger to leave the train at Killarney. A few days before, a political meeting had been held there with a deal of disturbance, but now the drab town was quiet and the empty hotels seemed to watch me with pathetic inviting eyes. In the private hotel at Muckross, there was only an old maid and her cat beside myself. A man in knickerbockers came in every hour or so to tipple alone in the parlour. The landlady seemed to live in a dream of the peaceful past, sighing for those summers of innumerable English tourists. Beyond the woods, the Upper Lake gleamed or darkened with showers around its islets and, as I walked along the road

156

towards the water, there was no sound but the chirping of fledglings and I thought it like the clink of half-crowns and shillings in my pocket. When the moon rose on the edge of night above the May woods, I thought again of that strange poem of James Cousins. As I lay in bed, I heard men arguing over the newspaper beneath my window.

A few days later I stayed in lodgings in a side-street in the town. It was owned by two young women in their late thirties and every night when I was going to bed the elder one came into the room and talked to me. She was fair-haired and still good-looking. In a mysterious tone she told me that there was a bad house next door and that in the past British soldiers used to go there. Every night she talked of the bad house as if she had brooded over it for years. I was tempted to lay her down gently on the bed, but I was too shy.

So every day I cycled for miles to the Gap of Dunloe, Aghadoe and other places, excited, wondering to myself why she talked so much of the bad house and hoping that I would have more courage when she sat on my bed at night and talked in her low dreamy voice.

A week later I pedalled along the sea-road to Dingle. Barefoot children hurried hand in hand from the little school-house; women in fringed black shawls passed by with baskets; men were gathering seaweed in creels and driving their laden asses along the boreens. The road had been trenched in several places, bridges blown up and the carts had to go down by the shore when the tide was out. There were only commercial travellers staying at the hotel in Dingle and they spoke uneasily of one who had been robbed the week before of £20 at Connor's Pass, a blind corner among the hills. These townsmen spoke of the Troubles, not with the vehemence that wearied us in Dublin, but with what seemed apathy. This generation had done enough, they said, and spoke with hope of lands that might come back to their families. In the little bar that night we talked not of Civil War but about drink and the mountainy places beyond Ventry. The man behind the counter who had been to the United States leaned over and said to me, 'You must go to Dunquin. They have the best Irish. In fact they all talk like poets over there.'

As I cycled with the breeze along the peninsula, all the men hurried from the little stony fields and called out to me in Irish.

'Is there a coming together? Is there peace yet?'

They went back shaking their heads when I said there was not. I

157

came at last to Slea Head and saw the Blasket Islands and, far away across the ocean, the jagged pinnacles of the Skelligs where hermits had their cells for half a century in the early Christian age. Feeling hungry, I stopped at a miserable cottage and asked in Irish for food. The man and barefoot woman brought me into the dark kitchen in which there was scarcely any furniture. The woman made strong tea for me – milkless – and gave me slices of griddle bread without butter, a plateful of salty dulse. I was stricken with pity for the poverty of these, the last speakers of the Irish language, and offered them some money but they refused to take any. It was only with much difficulty that they would let me give a florin to one of their ragged little children who were staring at me in wonder, big-eyed.

When I came to the market town of Tralee, I put up at a cheap inn where drovers stayed. I had hardly put a foot inside the door when two young men entered, questioned me closely and then went out into the hall to examine my bicycle. The daughter of the house looked at me suspiciously when they had gone and after I had finished my tea of bacon and eggs, I hurried down to the local barracks where I complained to the Gardai, pointing out that the people at the inn had given me queer looks since the young men called. The Gardai told me that they were looking for a bank robber but they had rung up Killarney and I was not the man. They promised that they would tell the people at the inn and when I came back a guard came to explain so that all was well again. That evening the old woman who owned the doss-house talked to me of the Troubles, of the burning of her son's shop, the searching of her house, the volleys night after night in the town. She crooned to herself. 'This beautiful country of ours, this beautiful country of ours!' Her voice lingered and caressed the words. I had never before seen old age so beautiful and so serene and as she crooned to herself, she seemed to me like Kathleen Ni Houlihan with white hair.

When I got to my room I found that everything was rickety and the small window stuck, but, thinking of the old woman, I forgave all. In two ticks my clothes were off and I was fast asleep for I had ridden sixty miles that day from Dingle over Conor Pass and down the eastern side of the promontory. In the morning, when I woke, I felt several bites and, jumping up, pulled back the worn counterpane to find that the bottom sheet was black with thousands of fleas. I thought of the guest-house in Cork and of the play I had written

158

about the medieval, wandering scholar and poet, Anier MacConglinne, who had lain down supperless among as great a multitude. When I came down to breakfast, I saw the old woman in a corner of the room but, remembering those hundreds of hoppers, I grimly avoided her eyes and after breakfast, paid the bill, wheeled out my bicycle, jumped on to the saddle.

That evening as I was on my way back to Killarney, I heard the pleasant sound of a melodeon from a small house by the roadside. Several young men with Colt revolvers ran out and cried: 'Halt!' They questioned me sharply but I replied in Irish and, much embarrassed, they shook their heads. So I upbraided them sternly in English. At last they let me go but I had scarcely cycled half a mile when I heard a shout. Two of the fellows, heads down, were cycling after me. They raised their heads and waved to me to stop. They brought me back and I waited outside the house while the officer in command was dancing inside. After a quarter of an hour, girls, flushed from the dancing, came out and sat on the grass in the sun, but they turned their heads away from me. I stared uncomfortably at the grey haze of the MacGillycuddy Reeks fifteen miles away. When the melodeon stopped, the officer came out, a gun stuck in his belt. He was not satisfied. What was I doing in Kerry? I told him that I had come to write poetry there and that visitors should not be treated in this way. He replied that I would have to come back to Killorglin with him and his men after the dance. I saw in my mind's eye the townspeople at their doors watching the prisoner being brought in without knowing that a mistake had been made. I could not return there to see Puck Fair in the Autumn when the tinkers gather and Kerry people come from all parts of the Kingdom to drink and make merry in the bars and behind the ditches for a week. I turned to the young man, while the girls still sat in the sunlight with averted heads listening to every word.

'You must technically arrest me and then take the legal consequences of a mistake.' I used large words to impress him. The commandant hesitated, fingering his revolver. At last he ordered his men to release me and I cycled off, still uneasy, knowing that I would pass other wayside cottages, hear the melodeon as other young men and girls were dancing reel or twostep inside.

It was so cool and shadowy under ash and elm that I almost thought rain-clouds were hurrying once more from the south-west. But no shower danced drearily among the leaves as I wandered on that summer's day along a woodland path through the great demesne at Birr. Gradually I realized that the path was not as simple as it seemed; indeed, it was guileful and ingenious as a maze. I found myself tramping across rustic bridges, gliding past holly and laurel, or lingering between light and shade at the riverside. A minute or two later there was only a gleam of water among the distant trees; but I knew that I would find the river again at the next corner. That wild river seemed in this secluded demesne to be on its best behaviour. Was it, indeed, the same river which I had seen in the town of Birr, creeping dirtily over a weir and disgracing itself on a mudbank beneath tumblesome walls and old eighteenth-century houses? Clearly, in all this apparent wilderness of trees and waters there was some plan.

Very soon I passed a few wood-cutters leaning around a small fire of twigs and eating their mid-day meal, and I realized that they had been lopping untidy branches. I heard a clink on a grassy bank after that, and met an old man sharpening his scythe. Suddenly the woods came to an end, and I was out once more in the sunlight. In front of me was a lake, tastefully ornamented with water lilies, and in one clear reach of water, beneath the shade of overhanging boughs, wild duck were swimming up and down.

I passed a grove and came to the central parkland. At a little distance was a keep, but only two of the castellated walls were standing. Was it one of those unfinished follies which defy the plans of architects? Suddenly I knew that I had seen this strange watch-tower before, and, flashing with excitement and certainty, my memory shot into the past. The great gun. . . . From the earth to the moon. . . . Jules Verne. Once more I could see that illustration of a strange tower in the story by Jules Verne; I could almost read with my mind's eye the words underneath it: 'The Giant Telescope at Birr or Parsonstown'. But surely in that illustration there were elaborate galleries of wrought iron around the tower, and above them loomed the dark cap of the telescope. I had forgotten all about that monster telescope at Birr, which had been world-famous in the middle of the last century. Schoolboys are always excited by the mechanical triumphs of invention, and I had felt a patriotic pride in the fact that our little country possessed the largest reflecting telescope in the world.

The greenland was so smooth that I hesitated to trespass on it. But there was nobody in sight, and so I stole across the grass. I must be right, for the lofty wall of the tower could not be more than a century old, and no ivy had been permitted to cling there. I turned the corner, and, to my astonishment, saw a black object protruding from the ground; the telescope was still there.

As speedily as a schoolboy, I dashed round and saw, with a shock, that fallen giant. There, indeed, jutting from a pit between the two walls, was the mighty shell of the telescope, pointing no longer to the heavens, but the distant woodland. The glorified object of my early dreams met disconcerting reality. Truth to tell, this crumbling wonder of the scientific world looked like a vast canister with the lid off, the clumsy funnel of 'The Great Eastern' and its dangerous rake even suggested a home-made howitzer. The shell was made of deal, clasped with iron hoops and smeared with old tarry paint, and all around it were convolvulus and the merry heads of flowering weeds. I peered into the pit, and, among the nettles, I could see rusting cogwheels and axles.

I could not but gaze with reverence and sorrow at the remains of what had once been one of the wonders of the world. Here the earl-astronomer had waited on his chilly iron gallery until the constellations crossed the meridional line. In the gleaming speculum below he had seen, frail as mortal breath, the haze of the nebulae. Man contemplates the heavens with awe and faith, seeing nothing but his own ignorance or vanity. Yet, with some tin, copper and a few poisons, he can fashion a polished metal and find some of the long-withheld secrets of the universe.

I turned away in some melancholy from the monumental ruin, but not without consoling thoughts. Surely the simple hands which had ached to uproot those flowering weeds and nettles had been restrained by a sense of mystery and awe. Piety itself, I thought also, had left the empty shell of that world-famous telescope to the gentleness of time and our soft Irish rain.

'You never saw so many people in your life. They come from all parts of the country, far and wide, to make the pilgrimage,' said the old man, who pointed out to me the track along the slope of Croagh Patrick. He spoke so eloquently about the great annual pilgrimage to the Reek, that it was with difficulty I ventured at last to glance at my watch and leave him. But his words had cast a lingering spell over my mind, and, as I hurried up the furzy slopes and scrambled along the short-cuts, my solitary mood was disturbed. I seemed to hear the shrill whistle of excursion trains coming into Westport, the grinding of motor brakes down at Murrisk, the jingle of harness, the faint whirr of innumerable bicycle wheels. But as I stared at the long, distant ridge of Croagh Patrick, I forgot the reverential crowds who climbed there on one Sunday in the year. A small misty cloud hid the upper part of the mountain, but it disappeared in a few minutes, and I saw the chapel on the summit, outlined like a tiny square cairn against the sky.

Suddenly, as I came over a few tumbled rocks, there stretched before me the narrow track of shale. Ridge beyond ridge, that clear, steep track rose before me, and there was something very familiar about it to me. I realized that it was, indeed, the straight and narrow path known to us all from age-old allegory and homily. I was glad that I was making the pilgrimage alone, and not scrambling up the loose shale among the murmurs of a multitude of pilgrims. Looking down, I could see the little promontory at Murrisk, with its sparse, ancient trees and its ruined abbey. Island beyond island, the narrow runs of Clew Bay glittered in the morning sunlight as I climbed higher. The legendary reach of ocean below me in the west brought back to my mind the traditional stories of Granuaile. She had rebelled not only against the insolent rule of the stranger, but against the laws of matrimony. She had taken to the sail and roamed the liberal seas with strong men.

Realizing that such thoughts should not be entertained by a pilgrim, I determined not to look down at Clew Bay any more, and so I cast my eyes modestly on the ground. Scarcely had I done so when I found myself staring at a small and unexpected object. It was a dainty wooden heel wrenched from a girl's shoe. What pretty foot from Dublin had been supported by that little object before me?

I thought of the young girl-pilgrim hobbling up the track on one heel, her vanity completely chastened. My thoughts were becoming distracted again, and I hastened on. But to my astonishment, I found that the way was strewn with shoe-heels. Can no exhortations prevent women from raising their stature a couple of inches in order to reach men's hearts? It seemed as if the very ground itself had protested and wrenched away these objects of folly.

In order to escape from my own indignation, I looked determinedly at the rocks on each side of the track. My astonishment was increased even more when I noticed that here and there, hidden discreetly in chink or lying in the open, with rackish necks, was a great number of bottles. As I struggled along, those abandoned bottles began to afflict me with a thirst which was as great as my curiosity about them. Were bona fide travellers, overcome by sudden remorse, accustomed to struggle up to the slope of the historic mountain and collapse among its rocks? Suddenly a satisfactory explanation of the mystery flashed into my mind. The travellers in Lord Dunsany's play *The Glittering Gate* are tantalized on their journey to heaven in a very effective way. Innumerable bottles descend within hand's reach through the abyss, but when the travellers grasp them, all prove to be empty. Had some zealous and practical soul-saver placed those empty beer bottles there in order to make the straight and narrow way more arduous for the male pilgrims?

Amid these distractions and temptations of thought, I scarcely knew that the sunlight was gone until I noticed the shale gleaming wetly at my feet. A fine drizzle was racing down towards the hollows from which I had come, racing so lightly, so delicately, I knew that I was walking through a cloud. In the chill twilight of that cloud, sound had become strange as if it were trying to hush itself. The loose stones and gravel no longer clinked and rattled from my boots. They fell down with a mournful, solemn sound. In the loneliness of that cloud I became aware at last of remote centuries. It may have been along this traditional track that St. Patrick had climbed to the mountain top in order to begin his great fast. I could only see a few yards ahead of me into the deepening gloom. The rapid mist, so fine that it scarcely wet my shoulders, sped downwards. But when I looked back, the glimmering shale ended abruptly in a swirling gloom.

I came at last to a great jutting rock. Far below that sudden cliff might be the Hollow of the Demons. This might be the very spot where Patrick had wrestled with the powers of darkness. Tireachan tells us that the demons and evil spirits first came in the form of enormous black birds. But the grave bellringer drove them back with a clapper. They returned again in greater numbers, running on the air in half-human, half-bestial shape, to confound their antagonist. I crept cautiously towards the cliff:

> But as I stumbled to the flint
> Where blessed Patrick drove a crowd
> Of fiends that roared like cattle-men,
> Until they stamped themselves out
> Between the fiery pens, I felt
> Repentance gushing from the rock.

Spiritually fortified, overcoming the ache of mortal muscle, I struggled on through the glimmer and gloom, knowing that I must now be near the top of the mountain. The mist had become thicker, the track was steeper, and, as I stopped anxiously for a moment, I thought I heard the first mutterings of storm. But I was determined to reach the peak. The track turned and came to an end and I groped bewildered across finer gravel and turf. Peering through the mist, I saw at last the plain concreted wall of the small church. Stone by stone, the material for that holy edifice had been carried up the mountain track.

I groped around the walls until I came to the simple door. It was locked, but there was an inscription painted on it. Greatly moved, I stumbled forward across loose stones. What words, the highest in Ireland, would I find here, inscribed in the clouds, for the edification and spiritual refreshment of the solitary pilgrim? Here on this desolate peak, where our national saint fasted for forty days and nights in wind, rain and tempest, I read in large, white-painted letters the one word: 'Offerings'. Under that legendary word was a slot in the locked door. Fumbling in my pocket, I drew out the poet's mite – a penny. But scarcely had I dropped it into the money-box when I leaped back in alarm. For suddenly, as if that small coin had magnified itself a hundred times and had awakened as many echoes, it clattered and reverberated through the empty church. The reverberations did not cease – they seemed to rumble and spread through the misty darkness around me. Terrified by the prodigious consequences of my action, I fled down the mountain track, and it was not until I came to the cliff above the Hollow of Demons that I realized a thunderstorm had broken around the mountain's top.

Twenty Two

THERE ARE VERY FEW long narrative poems in modern Irish literature. Yet the most original and strongest of them all is practically unknown. We have very few lyrical ballads, yet the finest of them remains unread and its music sings into silence.

> From Youghal, where gulls take harbour,
> Youghal, the strand of yews,
> We stood away off Brandon,
> Three nights out on the cruise.

Deirdre Wed and *The Rock of Cloud* were written by the County Cork poet, Herbert Trench. But the name of Herbert Trench will not be found in any of our Irish books of reference. Ernest Boyd, Stephen Gwynn, Professor Morton, and M. Rivoallan, whose *Littérature Irlandaise Contemporaine* was published just before the war, do not seem to have heard of him. So much for the knowledge and acumen of our literary historians and self-appointed chroniclers!

Neglect affords us at least the dubious pleasure of making discovery for ourselves. Late on a winter's evening, when I was a student, I happened to be looking haphazardly through some books in an obscure corner of a public library. I came upon one entitled *Deirdre Wed and Other Poems*, by Herbert Trench. The book had been published in 1901, half a dozen years or more before Yeats and Synge wrote their plays about Deirdre. I opened the book at the tenth page and instantly became a captive, for a strange, furious voice from the remote past whirled beyond bookcounter and shelf:

> Is this bed my work?
> Nay – too great clearness underneath the thunder

Shew'd insupportably the things to be.
Too long have I, with glamours, drops and runes,
Shook round her cabin low my skirts of storm
To shield thee from that devastating face.

In great agitation I paid my book fines and made off with the small green volume. Instead of the muted music of the Celtic Twilight, I held in my fist 'a mad discordancy, like fifes, drums, brasses'. I stopped outside shop windows in Bolton Street, leaned against lamp-posts, pleasing my brain with the concussion of fine words. For many months I knew that some day I must meet Herbert Trench. But he was living in retirement near Florence. Meanwhile bullets whistled across the Liffey and armoured cars rattled through the Dublin streets.

I arrived in Florence three weeks before the sudden death of the poet. He was living alone in an old Renaissance villa of palatial proportions outside the city, somewhere near Settignano. I was brought by an elderly Italian housekeeper through a great mirrored hall or ballroom. The hall was chill, melancholy and empty but for a Mercury of ancient patina. I learned later that this bronze figure had been found by the poet himself at Pompeii. I followed the old woman down corridors, up short flights of steps, until we came to a small library, cool and pleasant with reflected light.

To my surprise the poet was lying ill in bed in a corner of the room. He welcomed me instantly and thrust aside all mention of his illness. He had been suffering, as he explained, from nose-bleeding. But the sight of compresses, stained with his blood, filled my mind with faintness and an uneasy sense of foreboding. I glanced out of the window from time to time, as we talked, and saw across the Plain of Lombardy the towers and domes of Florence. But in my mind I saw those gloomy Connemara glens under Muilrea and Bengorm, where the poet had found his first inspiration. In great bewilderment I gradually realized that he had forgotten his early poetry and was completely possessed by the urgency of his present idea.

'I never forgot my first visit to Italy,' he exclaimed, 'the memory, of it remained for many years in my mind like a burning dream.'

The phrase held my attention and I remembered the concluding lines of his epic fragment. Once more I saw Deirdre and her lover free at last from all pursuit:

And like a burning dream the host, dissolving,
Pass'd. On the pale bank not a torch remain'd.
They looked on one another, left alone.

But the poet could not guess my thoughts, for he was talking rapidly and was so isolated from me by his mood that I could watch his noble acquiline features. I could not grasp the philosophical system which he had evolved for himself because, like that of Bergson, it seemed to depend on images, but I realized its serenity and fortitude. I knew then that he had long since passed into that 'Italian light' from which Yeats had fled in his earlier years.

I followed the silent housekeeper once more through the shadowy mirrored hall. Had I been wrong in my youthful enthusiasm, and was an extreme indulgence in speculative thought the last pleasure which all good poets must seek on earth?

For a fortnight I went out, as often as I dared, to see Herbert Trench, but I could never get him to speak of his early work – and so I never told him why I had come to Italy. I think he must have been lonely, for he wrote several letters to me filled with the excitement of his last thoughts. He had followed Matthew Arnold as inspector of English schools, and, as manager of the Haymarket Theatre, had fought the commercialism of the London stage. His one bitter regret was that, in the rash confidence of early manhood, he had given to public affairs too much of the time needed by poetry.

On the evening of my last visit, Herbert Trench had recovered from his illness, and he came to show me a short-cut, so that I might not miss the little tram to Florence. As the tram rattled and clanked beyond the vineyards he insisted, on running with me, despite my anxious expostulations. I can still see him at the corner of that shadowy laneway in the light of the tram, mopping his brow with a bandana, and then waving to me like a great schoolboy. Next morning he set out for Boulogne, the scene of his play on Napoleon. A week later, news came that he was dead.

II

One morning in Maytime, Angela and I took the tram from Florence for we had planned to spend a day in the pinewoods beyond Fiesole.

She was a young artist on her way to Rome and we had only met a fortnight before. We had with us in a rustic basket a long baton of bread, slices of salami, cheese and a big flask of Chianti. The tram was filled with elderly English ladies and rattled along the curving rails up the hill road. As we passed Settignano, Angela pointed out to me at some distance on the left the Poggio Gherardo. I remembered Boccaccio's description of that delicious suburban retreat on the top of a hill, with its loggias, hall, many rooms, all of them ornamented with jocund paintings; outside were a terraced garden, wells of coldest water, topiary yews. I thought of the graceful Pamponea crowned with bay leaves from the garden, Lauretta, Pamfilio, Dineo and the other gay young revellers and ladies who had fled from the dire plague in Florence. On the second day, that pleasant company, with their lutes and song books, walked in the cool of the evening to stay at the Villa Palmieri. The villa was surrounded by pergolas of vines, thickets of jasmin and crimson roses, carved marble fountains with recumbent nymphs and satyrs. On the way, the ladies had stopped to bathe and disport themselves in the river.

Into my mind came trooping those tales of graceful lie-a-beds, who gazed admiringly at their gallants in short cloak and hose with rapiers and jewelled daggers. I thought of the story of the Mother Superior who, hearing giggling, had hurried from her cell and caught a young nun in the very act of darkness. By mistake, instead of her coif, she had whipped up the breeches of a canon whom she had been entertaining in her cell. The pretty sinner, hiding her cropped head and impudently fastening her placket hole, pointed out to the assembled community the leather pair of breeches dangling round the neck of the Reverend Mother, and so escaped punishment. I thought of Agilafe's wife who rode twice with her groom late at night and of the liaison of Salvestra and Givolamo, which had so tragic an ending, and I thought of the wife of Master Mazzeo, who gave her husband an opiate in syrup and then opened an ornamental chest, in which her young lover was hidden. Then there was the demoiselle who slept until the cheeping of dawn with a nightingale clasped in her hand; all the household stole into her room to see that pretty sight. Chaucer had taken stories from the *Decameron* and spoiled them with English coarseness.

Then with many a jest and laugh at the simplicity of the friar and many a flout at the distaff-ful's and combs and cards, they solaced themselves with one another to their no small delight. Nor did they omit so as to arrange matters that they were well able to dispense with Master Friar, and yet pass many another night together with no less satisfaction: to which goal I pray that I, and all other Christian souls that are so minded, may be speedily guided of God and His holy mercy.

Those medieval tales disturbed my mind and I dismissed them hastily from the tram.

Angela had been friendly with D. H. Lawrence for a little while when he was in Italy and the Master had instructed her in the pagan mysteries of love. She explained to me that lovers took part in a solemn rite of sacrifice in the Temple of Eros among incense, wreaths and rose petals. The unselfishness of that doctrine delighted me and I longed to prostrate myself with her on the invisible altar.

The tram passed the monastery on the hill at Fiesole and stopped at the small paven square which once had been a Roman encampment. We alighted with all the English ladies and sat outside a cafe on iron seats drinking coffee.

Then we set out eagerly along the mountain road to the pinewoods and there, among rock roses, we sought shade and opened the basket. Silently, after our repast, Angela stood up and much to my surprise, began to take off her clothes. They might have been Greek robes as she stepped from them and I saw for the first time her noble breasts, her thighs and adorable *toison*. We lay on the invisible altar, half aware of the incense rising up, the scattering petals, and after we had communed with the god, we lingered in each other's arms and dreamed.

III

So, for several weeks, we sought the pinewoods, then, in order that we might meet more frequently. I stayed at a cheap trattoria in the Piazza at Fiesole. My bedroom had an iron balcony from which I could look down at the Plains of Lombardy.

One day, as I sat in the small public park, I forgot the hour and

170

found that the gates had been locked. I climbed a sloping rampart to the monastery above and dropped down on the far side. A stout young monk was carrying a crisp lettuce on a platter along an arcade. He stopped at a hatch to hand it in to another monk in the refectory. In halting Italian, I explained my plight to the monk. He listened and then said abruptly: 'Capisco'. He pointed out to me in ill-humour the way to the main gate.

That afternoon as I watched far below the Duomo, the Palazzo Vecchio and the windings of the River Arno, the sky darkened suddenly, thunder rolled, lightning flashed, criss-crossed above the plains and a downpour hit the city.

I sat, miserable in my thoughts, wondering how I could spend the two idle hours before supper on such an afternoon, for Angela would not be able to come up from Florence. To my surprise, there was a knock at my bedroom door. Dropping my empty notebook, I ran to open it. Angela streamed in, her raincoat pooling the floor-tiles, her storm-blown hair in wisps and piggie-wiggie tails. I wrapped her in a bath towel and dried her tenderly, kissing all her dampness. As we lay in bed, the window knob rattled, the lattices creaked. I fancied between our kisses that the Thunderer of the ancient world was displaying his strength to Mietis, Themis, Eurynome, Latina, Danae, Leda, Aegina or Alemena. Only Europa frowned as the god hurled bolt after bolt across unmapped latitudes far beyond the Pillars of Hercules.

Twenty Three

I

DURING MY FIRST WEEKS in London, I met by chance several writers who had disappeared from public notice at the close of the 'nineties. One afternoon, I left *The Six Bells* in Chelsea where I had been drinking mild-and-bitter, with an acquaintance. We went to an art exhibition given by a young Scottish artist of the Modernist school. In his painting he used only the colours of the spectrum. As I moved slowly among the crowd, the red, orange, yellow, green, blue, indigo cubes were confused blurs. In the far corner I was introduced to the Comtesse de Brémont, a thin elderly lady, who talked to me tenderly of her old friend Oscar Wilde. As we swayed towards each other, I realized that she was as drunk as I was. Unfortunately, I forgot at once the anecdotes which she related to me. Three weeks later, she was found dead in her lodgings: according to the Coroner, her death was due to semi-starvation.

A small group of little-known poets met once a month in the basement kitchen of a flat near Earls Court owned by Henry Simpson, a bald-headed Scotsman who was, like Samuel Rogers, a poet and bank manager. I was invited there and putting on my old-fashioned velvet jacket, my large flowing tie, arrived punctually at 8 p.m. I thought the poems read out were indifferent, and, being young and confident, was certain that I would make an impression. But the two lyrics which I read out were received without comment, and in dejection I went back to my warm place near the closed range. Tea was made and amidst the general conversation I sat alone. A small dapper man with a cravat and monocle came over to me: 'Are you the young Yeats redivivus?' he asked with a smile. Then he added with a slight bow. 'I am Victor Plarr'.

I was astonished for I had believed that he was long since dead. F. R. Higgins and I had read his short biography of his friend Ernest Dowson, the first of its kind, and we often quoted with mock gravity a sentence from it.

'When a poet dies, I always send a laurel wreath.'

We admired his epigrammatic lines about Mabel Beardsley who was more courageous than her brother:

Epitaphium Citharistriae

Stand not uttering sedately
Trite oblivious praise about her!
Rather say you saw her lately
Lightly kissing her last lover.

Whisper not 'There is a reason
Why we bring her no white blossom';
Since the snowy bloom's in season,
Strow it on her sleeping bosom:

Oh! for it would be a pity
To o'erpraise her or to flout her;
She was wild, and sweet, and witty,
Let's not say dull things about her.

Yeats, if I am right, owed something to this poem when he wrote *Upon a Dying Lady*.

Sometime later, I was invited by a young poet, Edward Davidson, to his flat in Shepherd's Bush. He was Literary Editor of an Anglican periodical and frequently gave me books to review. As soon as I pressed the bell, the door opened and my host greeted me. The small white hall, dazzling with electric light, was packed with writers, including J. B. Priestley, W. J. Turner, Ralph Hodgson, without his dogs on leash. Davidson made a short speech of welcome and on behalf of the English poets and novelists there presented me with a token of their regard. I found myself clutching a strange object. I glanced down at an obscene knob, shiny with varnish, between my finger and impudent with green ribbon. Slowly I realized that it was one of those shillelaghs which are sold in Dublin gift shops to tourists. I should have leaped into the drawing room and, whirling it around my head, trolled that well-known ballad *The Humours of Donnybrook Fair*.

'Tis there are dogs dancing and wild beasts a-prancing.
With neat bits of painting in red, yellow and gold,
Toss-players and scramblers, and showmen and gamblers,
Pickpockets in plenty, both of young and of old.
There are brewers, and bakers, and jolly shoemakers,
With butchers and porters, and men that cut hair;
There are mountebanks grinning, while others are singing
To keep up the humours of Donnybrook Fair.

Unfortunately, my face became so long, that the practical joke sneaked away and hid in a corner for the rest of the night.

Only later did I hear that Edward Davidson had spent a day searching in gift shops, for the dreadful trophy. That evening I felt that I could not succeed in London, since writers there had still the Victorian view of Ireland.

II

'Did we talk about anything? Of course we did. Tolstoi and his doctrine of celibacy. Ibsen's Hedda. Strindberg's view of the female animal. And we agreed that Friedrich Nietzsche appealed to us immensely.'

In that way spoke the daring young heroine of *Now Spring has come* and she was the first to refer to Nietzsche in the English language. The sentence is from a short story by Miss Mary Dunne, an Irish writer, born in Australia, who gained a brief celebrity in the Yellow Book Period. Miss Dunne chose the pseudonym of 'George Egerton' for her first collection of short stories, *Keynotes*, which was published by John Lane in 1894, and needless to say, the title-page design was by Aubrey Beardsley. The international vogue of 'George Egerton' can easily be understood, for her themes were sophisticated and their milieu was cosmopolitan, Norway, London, Paris, Holland, Ireland. Moreover, these short stories were psychological studies, experiments in a free form, which had rid itself of the exigencies and falsifying tendencies of plot. They revealed the New Woman, not yet content to abandon mystery, charm, or even naughtiness, and appropriately, their style was witty, incisive and yet lyrical, when necessary, in mood.

Occasionally, 'George Egerton' glanced back severely at the middle-class life which she had known in Ireland, but in only one story did she use a complete Irish theme, exemplifying the subjection of woman. She anticipated in it the realism of a later generation and gave us the first glimpse of Night-town. In this short story of the Dublin slums, she describes a woman hurrying from the brothel district to the Pro-Cathedral, searching in vain for a priest at midnight, willing to come to see a dying prostitute. The background against which the tragedy is set has a lurid quality typical of the 'nineties. It is the night of a distillery fire and along the gutters ten-year old whisky runs in flames, watched by a tormented, ragged crowd. Beyond the roof-tops the sky glows.

I was introduced to 'George Egerton' by Louis McQuilland, an Irish journalist and book-reviewer who lived with his elderly sister in a flat above a shop in the King's Road, Chelsea. Every Sunday, writers and visitors, on their way to or from Ireland, gathered in his cheerful drawing-room and when there was a crowd, the late-comers sat on the floor. Louis McQuilland was proud of his remarkable likeness to Disraeli and furthered it by wearing always a stock and choker. At the time, the Sitwells were disturbing the reviewers by experiments in poetic ragtime and other imaginative novelties. The Irish critic attacked them wildly in *The Daily Express* and received a few days later a long congratulatory letter from Bournemouth. In reply, he wrote an equally long, indiscreet letter to his unknown correspondent. Several other letters were exchanged. At the end of a month, McQuilland's letters were returned to him with a brief note. The letters from Bournemouth had been written by Miss Edith Sitwell, then transcribed and posted by a former butler at Renshaw Hall. When Osbert Sitwell published an amusing caricature of McQuilland in *Triple Fugue*, his victim began to suffer from delusions. He told us that the irate poet had pushed him off the footpath just outside his hall door. The illusion was so strong that he feared to go out for his short stroll before lunch, along the King's Road to the World's End, ebony walking stick beneath his arm, trilby aslant.

On a wintry week-evening, I left my backroom in a slummy side-street off the King's Road and went round to see Louis McQuilland

and to warm myself at his fire. There was a grey-haired lady in her sixties with him and he introduced her to me as Mrs. Golding Bright, better known as 'George Egerton'. As she was leaving, she invited me to come and see her.

So, once a week, I stepped into the lift at the mansion flats in Ridgeway Gardens, near Tottenham Court Road. 'George Egerton' always wore a black dress, much décolleté for she was obviously proud of her ample maternal bosom. To keep my eyes from the firm milk-white curves, I had to avert my glance frequently as she talked. Moreover, the quick, piercing glances which darted from her rimless glasses were as disconcerting. She told me much about the 'nineties. During an inspired summer at Millstreet in County Cork, she had completed *Keynotes*. In London, because of its immediate success, she met Aubrey Beardsley, Henry Hartland, Richard Le Gallienne, G. B. Shaw, Yeats, John Davidson, Max Beerbohm, Lily Langtry and others.

Yeats has left no record of his many meetings with her. No doubt, as a young poet brooding over his twilight lyrics and his prose tales, legendary and Rosicrucian, he felt there was no place for cosmopolitan womankind in the Irish literary revival. The art of the revivalists must be sophisticated, but the themes were to be traditional and rural.

'George Egerton' spoke with dislike of the posing of Yeats, but I suspect that she was attracted to him at first by his strangeness. They had met at a party in Fitzroy Square. The folding doors between the two drawing-rooms were open and the inner room was empty. A young man appeared from nowhere in the back room, dressed in a black velvet jacket with a large flowing black tie. He stood staring at the wall as if in a trance. Soon the guests were whispering, wondering who the remarkable-looking stranger could be. When curiosity had increased sufficiently, the young Irish poet came forward with a smile to greet his hostess.

On another occasion at a small party in Fitzroy Square, Yeats was telling stories about the fairies. Suddenly he peered down at the threadbare rug before the fender and, in a chanting tone, murmured: 'I see an abyss and far down in it is a hawk with poised wings'.

'I can see nothing,' complained his sceptical compatriot, noticing a large hole in the rug.

During the period of *The Yellow Book*, the poet of the Celtic

Twilight lived abstemiously, while Lionel Johnson, Ernest Dowson and poet-companions in the Rhymer's Club were drinking themselves into the other world. 'George Egerton' assured me, however, that when he came to her flat in Battersea, then a Bohemian quarter, the picturesque poet ate steak and onions or a couple of chops with considerable relish.

In a letter, dated February 9, 1939, she wrote to a young cousin, Terence de Vere White, who lived in Dublin: 'I could write a queer memory – won't. Would have to be a bit malicious in the French sense. Yeats had supper at my flat one Sunday night, a conventional Sunday, cold beef, pickled and beer, ate heartily and tossed his locks (black then), flung out his arms and said, 'I smell a smell, a dire dank smell'. 'If you do', said I, 'it's psychic or comes from yourself, for I had the place tested before I brought Boy (her baby) 'into it.'

Despite his avoidance of black magic, Yeats was frequently aware of the presence of malodorous spirits.

'George Egerton' had spent a number of years with her second husband in Norway, where she met Ibsen and most of the younger writers. She translated *Hunger*, that grim story of a starving artist, by Knut Hamson. Unfortunately, the book attracted little attention and it was not until the early 'twenties that the sagas of the Norwegian novelist had a vogue in England. Later, I learned that, as a dark-haired young woman, 'George Egerton' had become his mistress for some time.

George Bernard Shaw feared the New Irishwoman, and at every social gathering he avoided her as much as he could, because of her sharp tongue, her witty retorts. Many years later, when Terence de Vere White was editing the letters of 'Aunt Chavelita' he wrote to the great man for information about her. G.B.S. had not forgotten the annoying way she had interrupted his monologues, for he replied volubly on a postcard of abuse: 'I remember G.E. (Mrs. G.B.) very well. She was so intolerably loquacious that she talked herself off the stage after she had won her way to the centre of it by her literary talent. It was incessant gabble, gabble, gabble, without any grace of address or charm of speech. Many sought to meet her once but not twice. There was nothing else to complain of. She was quite good-natured and well-meaning. Her loquacity was meant for companionableness but its excess undid her.'

Yet, at the time, Richard Le Gallienne and her publisher, John

Lane, were pursuing the emancipated young woman with dishonourable intentions!

The letters of Aunt Chavelita and the extracts from her Diaries, given by Terence De Vere White in his book, were frequently shrewd and incisive. Here is a reference to William Archer: 'Archer's veneration for Ibsen killed him in England as a playwright, otherwise he might be in repertory. Archer would translate 'Retire to Hades' when Ibsen frankly said 'Go to blazes'. In *Little Eyolf*, I think, he makes a character say, 'The champagne stood on the table and you tasted it not'. This was not Ibsen, it was a line out of a popular song, sung at the Tivoli in Copenhagen. Ibsen quoted it. 'I should have used boldly as my version a line out of a song sung by Marie Lloyd, that genius of vulgar wit and real music-hall artist.'

Here is a passing comment on *The Waste Land*: 'I don't grasp "Damp souls of housemaids". Their work is mostly dusty and the area is not their beat.'

I was suffering from deep depression since I had left Angela in Italy. Faint with the heavy and light fragrance of incense and of flowers, I had sacrificed myself with her for two weeks in Venice; waking in the darkness at night, we had lain in a still union until we reached the blessed state of Karezza. In my lodgings down a slum street off the King's Road, I thought of her as I turned the ardent pages of *Il Fuoco*, that novel in which d'Annunzio, unwearied of the pomegranate, had glorified his love for Eleanora Duse.

To distract me during that first winter in London, my sympathetic friend, Mrs. Golding Bright brought me once a week to a matinee in the West End. Plays of Somerset Maugham were on at several theatres and I saw with surprise the latest lighting and realistic sets, oriental markets, white archways, colourful stalls, against a sky-blue cyclorame. I saw the daughter of Madame Albanesi take the part of a Eurasian heroine in two of the plays. Many were enspelled by her low, husky voice, even though they knew this remarkable young actress was dying slowly of throat cancer.

R. Golding Bright, the third husband of 'George Egerton' was a small, quiet Englishman, one of the leading theatrical agents in London. Once his wife passed on to me his excellent suggestion that I should live in Oxford, where I would meet influential scholars instead of sitting on the floor in shabby studios in Chelsea. About the same time, Terence Grey, who had put on my first verse-comedy at the Festival Theatre, invited me down to Cambridge for a course of theatre. Unfortunately, I could not afford to leave London.

'George Egerton' had been converted, like many others, to the cause of Irish independence, by the events of the Rising, and she became well acquainted with the literary movement. She lent me books by neglected writers, including a collection of short stories by the composer Arnold Bax, who had lived for some years in Ireland and written under the pen-name of 'Dermot O'Byrne'. She lent me, also, that incomparable story by Seamus O'Kelly, *The Weavers Grave*, of which I had never heard.

In the Edwardian period, 'George Egerton' ceased publishing and her name was quickly forgotten. But her new interest in Irish affairs proved an inspiration. She wrote a group of stories about the country which have not appeared in print. One of them is topical in interest for it deals with the colour problem. A young Negro in the West Indies, a descendant of one of the Irish rebels sold into slavery in the Barbadoes during the Cromwellian period, was so stirred by the Rising, that he saved up enough money to visit the country of his ancestors. On his first day in Cork, he went into a public-house on the Coal Quay and got into conversation with some labourers who were drinking pints of Beamish there. They were flattered by his knowledge of the happenings of Easter Week.

'What's your name, sir?' one of them asked.

'Patrick Jeremiah O'Sullivan,' he replied proudly.

Believing that he was having a joke at their expense, the enraged workmen threw the unfortunate black man out into the street.

Among others whom I met at McQuilland's was the poet William Kean Seymour, who was contributing witty parodies at the time on English and Irish writers to *Punch*. There, also, I met Henry Savage, who had been a friend of that neglected poet and story-writer, Richard Middleton. At the beginning of the century, he had fought in the Boer War and joined up again when the Great War started. He told me that he had carried my first slim book of verse with him when he was in the trenches. He must have noticed my look of polite incredulity, for he brought, on the next Sunday, his muddied, battered copy to show me. Had it been a life-preserving Bible or prayerbook, with the usual bullet-dent in the cover, I could not have been more flattered.

179

One night, I met him at Piccadilly Circus in a shabby overcoat with a fur collar, looking more like a delapidated financier than a hard-up poet. As we watched the Rolls Royce cars glitter past, he exclaimed in his Cockney accent: 'They 'oite us, Clorke, the bourgeouisie 'oite us'.

One Sunday night I left that hospitable flat by chance with the young, fair-haired wife of an elderly artist. The stairs were in darkness and as we groped down them, I took her arm. We stopped against the wall on the left of the letter-box and before we knew what had happened our lips met in a long exquisite kiss. I suspected that Eros, remembering my sacrifices to him, was present in his Roman guise in order that he might show me how to escape from Imagination into the sunniness of Fancy. Soon, I would be playing quoits with Avril on happy afternoons, rolling a thin golden hoop with her, kissing her shoulder as she bent to feather the dart which she took from my quiver, or chasing blissfully with her after uncatchable butterflies.

Twenty four

AFTER THE FIRST GREAT WAR, J. C. Squire, Editor of *The London Mercury*, became the most powerful literary figure in Fleet Street. Every day at lunch hour, he came down the short flight of stairs from his office in Poppin's Court to the nearby tavern. He stood in a corner by the counter there, munching ham sandwiches, his tipple beside him. Among the constant writers and critics who surrounded him were Edward Shanks, Edmund Blunden, J. B. Priestley, 'Tommy' Pope, John Freeman, Alan Porter, Edward Davidson, J. M. Turner and H. M. Tomlinson. Stocky, red-farmer-faced, Hilaire Belloc arrived at times looking down contemptuously on all newcomers. Here was the most influential coterie in London and it was known jocosely to those who feared it as the Squirearchy. Its leader, who had assumed the manner and opinions of John Bull himself, was an outlander from Cornwall, but his crisp curled hair indicated, perhaps, Phoenician origin. Once a week, I climbed the stairs to the Editorial Office, or waited in the tavern, but failed to get a single book for review. However, after three months of faithful attendance, I was asked by Squire to write an article on the poetry of Herbert Trench.

Although the battle between the Ancients and Moderns was significant at the time, it has not been chronicled. The witty attacks by Lytton Strachey on the Eminent Victorians had prepared the way: quickly the Modernists captured important literary outposts and the assaults began. In his chilly, High Anglican tone, T. S. Eliot dismissed the criticism of Matthew Arnold. Ezra Pound, who was discovering for himself Troubadour song and Chinese poetry, whirled from his sling terrifying sentences in slang. The Poet Laureate was assailed regularly by young reviewers on their way down from Oxford and Cambridge. Cyril Connolly disposed of the popular lyrics of A. E. Housman in a clever essay which infuriated

E. V. Lucas and other traditionalists. In an historic phrase, a youngster – whose name I have forgotten – declared: 'We have removed Milton with a remarkable lack of fuss'.

The Georgian poets are still referred to as 'The Weekend School', and that belittling term is not inappropriate, for these writers did express the new age of the weekend motor drive and bus tour to Sussex or Margate. J. C. Squire wrote poems about winter-time in Battersea Park and football matches, poems which were deliberately muddied and oaf'd: in them he achieved a total effect of dullness. But in his narrative poem, *The Stockyard*, he wrote the grimmest and most realistic piece in the English language.

II

Robert Lynd, the Literary Editor of *The Daily News*, was the first to give me regular work, and I went up often in the clattering lift to his untidy office, with its piles of newspapers and books. He was too languid to raise his voice, and it was not easy to hear him as the printing machines in the basement rumbled with captions and shook the high premises.

It was difficult to reach the equally untidy den of Desmond MacCarthy in *The New Statesman* office in Queen's Street, for he was guarded and protected from his own generosity by his secretary, a handsome widow, known to all reviewers as the Dragon. Whenever I succeeded in dodging her, I came away with an armful of books. There was another difficulty. On the way up, I had to pass the Editorial door which was always ajar. Sometimes I could see Clifford Sharp in his room, glaring out at me from a drunken stupor. He was a brilliant, political journalist, and I feared, pitied him.

As Literary Editor, Desmond MacCarthy was always ready to try out a suggestion. On the shelves were hundreds of verse-books which had accumulated over several years; I offered to go through them in the hope of making some discoveries. Promptly, a crate arrived at my studio in Fulham. I spent a fortnight over the pile of hopes but was unable to find a single original line.

The weekly essays of Desmond MacCarthy were plain in style, but completely personal and frequently a humorous and electric figure of speech was to be found in them. For example, the enormous sociological novels of H. G. Wells in his Utopian phase are neatly summarized: 'His method of constructing a book was often just to take the back out of the cart of his mind, tilt up the shafts and let the contents fall with an exhilarating rumble'.

These easy-going essays were the result of hard, last-minute work and tension. One morning, when I called to his home in a leafy square, off the King's Road, he asked me to wait for a short while until he had finished his weekly article for *The Sunday Times*. He walked up and down the room, dictating to his secretary, stammering, pausing, weighing or changing his phrases, a look of torment, on his face, hands writhing. Suddenly, it was all over and we went out to lunch.

On another occasion, after dinner at his house, he talked all the evening about the novels of Henry James, whom he had known in his early years. It was almost midnight when I left, and it was doubtful whether I would reach Sloane Square Underground Station in time for the last train. My host insisted on walking along the Square with me. Suddenly he stopped near a lamp-post, stammering and writhing, one hand in his pocket as if he were dictating an article on Gissing. I waited somewhat alarmed until he said, 'Would . . . would you mind very much if I asked you to take a taxi?'

Promptly I pocketed the five shillings which he proffered so hesitantly to me, for I was then living in Finsbury, near the Seven Sisters' Road and had no wish to make that long journey on foot across half of London.

Leonard Woolf, the Literary Editor of *The Nation* in Great James' Street, was a complete contrast. In his dingy room in the return, he had two bookshelves, which he called respectively Hell and Purgatory. Over the door was a smaller one known as Heaven. Patiently, he considered the new review books, until the best of them were ranged on the shelf above the door ready for sending out.

One morning, I received an abrupt note from Desmond MacCarthy telling me that I must give him an immediate assurance in writing that I would cease to review books for *The Nation*. In reply, I refused to give any such undertaking unless I got a regular contract. Other reviewers also refused. Leonard Woolf sympathized with our fight for freedom and gave us as much additional work as he could in the columns of *The Nation*.

I have no doubt that Desmond MacCarthy had been compelled

to act in a way so uncharacteristic of him, for after a year, a book came to me from *The New Statesman*, with a slip of paper on which he had scribbled '600 words'. The battle was over.

The offices of *The Spectator* to which I also contributed were over a shop near the noisy corner of Covent Garden, and it was pleasant to look down on the lorries of vegetables, the stalls with their array of fruit and flowers. The poet, Alan Porter was the first Literary Editor there for whom I worked. When he left to settle down in the United States, the chair was warmed in rapid succession by an unusual number of posteriors (including a very pretty one). One afternoon, when I came into the office, I saw a large bronze Buddha on the editorial desk: sitting below it was a small cavalry officer, who had written a best-seller, the late Captain Yeates Brown. After he had left, the proprietors of *The Spectator* acquired a house in Gower Street. The parlour in which we waited politely downstairs was furnished with book-cases, lined with leather-bound volumes – suggestive of stability and of the Age of Steele and Addison. The Literary Editor's new office was a tiny maid's room in the return. In the Chair was a pleasant young man, just come down from College, sucking a new unfilled pipe – Peter Fleming. Others came and went, among them W. J. Turner. He had just published a collection of his difficult metaphysical poems. He greeted me enthusiastically and already I saw myself coming down the stairs every month with a bundle of books in gay wrappers. A week later the poet died suddenly. I did not return to the office any more.

III

For two years, I contributed to *T.P.'s Weekly*, which was published by the Amalgamated Press. The joint-Editors, Caradoc Evans and Con O'Leary, together with all their contributors, were regarded as intellectuals and avoided by the numerous Editors, who produced *Peg's Weekly*, novelettes, Comic Papers. There was a special official whose sole task was to make sure that Woman Editors did not use the words 'monthly' and 'ball' in the plural, because none of the Directors had the courage to tell them why.

Con O'Leary, a fine novelist, had worked on *The Manchester*

Guardian and at this time was 'ghosting' the memoirs of 'Tay Pay', for he had much knowledge of the history of the Irish party at Westminster. He got £250; the 'author' received £70,000.

Caradoc Evans was a burly peasant and native speaker of Welsh who frequently sang hymns with his compatriots at closing time. He had a strange vocabulary of four-letter compounds which affrighted strangers, and a habit of greeting all contributors with ambiguous questions such as: 'When did you last bury your rhubarb?'

The embarrassed caller was aware dimly of the obscene implication of these Colliery phrases.

Caradoc Evans had been a draper's assistant in Cardiff, exploited like many other young Welsh boys by the Welsh proprietors of great shops. He discovered the plays of Synge by chance and started to write short stories, getting his ironic effect by literal translation of words from the Welsh. When his play *Taffy* was produced in the West End, the Welsh dairy men in London rioted outside the Theatre and he became the National Enemy, so mordant was his satire on preachers and Bible men. His later stories, which are little known, are remarkable, for in them he brought the figures of folklore into the lives and houses of the folk, an imaginative method which was used also by the Irish dramatist, George Fitzmaurice, in the *Dandy Dolls* and other plays.

Soon I was working regularly, though unofficially, in the office. When the great printers' strike was over and the armoured cars gone, the Fleet Street proprietors transferred all their printing to the cheaper provincial presses. Printers who had worked hard and conscientiously for many years were flung out of employment. I remember of them, an elderly man who watched our copy for doubtful grammar. Frequently, Caradoc had brought me down to argue with him because I had an M.A. degree.

Messenger boys were sent twice a day from Watford to Fleet Street to collect copy and soon we were racing teams. Caradoc kept to the scissors and the pastepot, while Con and I tore a new biography or literary history in two, read hastily for anecdotes, interesting details, started to type the article, meeting somewhere in the middle as another messenger knocked at the door.

The problem of our drinking at lunch became an acute one, for rounds of mild-and-bitter dulled my mind. As I was earning a large amount of money, I suggested that we should try draught champagne although it was costly. Soon we were drinking a couple of bottles a day, in the underground wine-cellar, later bombed, at the corner of Ludgate Circus. The exhilaration was pleasant and the effects of dimness disappeared rapidly. Every Friday evening there was a pleasant custom: girl typists and secretaries sat in the wine-cellar, with a bottle of excellent Burgundy and a plate of biscuits on the small tables before them.

Frequently I wrote the leading article under the name of T. P. O'Connor, while he was taking a deserved rest from Parliamentary duties at Nice or Monte Carlo. Fortunately, his conversational style and personal tricks of speech were easy to copy.

Whenever *Mille Fleurs* drifted into the inner office in which Con and I were typing, half a book beside each of us, we knew that Caradoc's new mistress, a popular novelist in a large fur coat, was sitting by his desk. Once we heard voices raised. The door banged. His older mistress had found out, and when she seized the telephone receiver to ring up her rival, the alarmed Editor had snipped the wire with the scissors. He came in afterwards to us, with a dismal expression. How could he explain to the engineering staff the mystery of the cut wire? Despite the fact that he had to meet the amative demands of a large woman and a small one, Caradoc remained unsatisfied. His great wish was to have carnal knowledge of a woman doctor. Articles on medicine and home treatment were a feature of the periodical. In turn, attractive women doctors sat in his office, with tempting gun-metal-coloured stockings but all of them kept their elegant legs crossed.

Although I was earning about £1,000 a year, despite myself, the speed and tension became too much. I fled, exhausted, to Dublin. The next morning a telegram arrived from my distracted editor: 'Come back. More money. Caradoc.'

I could not resist his rustic plea. A few months later, the periodical stopped publication. We heard that the owners had decided that a weekly circulation of 72,000 copies was not enough.

186

Among new friends of mine was E. V. Odle, the editor of *The Argosy* magazine. I knew also his brother, a tall artist who wore his hair brushed down to his eyebrows. He illustrated Rabelais, *Les Contes Drolatiques* and other wicked works with superb immodesty. His wife was Dorothy Richardson who anticipated in her 'slow motion' novels the experiments of Joyce. They lived sparsely in a shack in Cornwall, rented it in summer and came to Bloomsbury where they smoked innumerable cigarettes.

E. V. Odle asked me to become Assistant Editor of *The Argosy* and a week or two later, I was appointed. The task of finding good stories in collections and files of old magazines was easy yet tantalizing, for the short story as a literary form is little more than a century old. We worked in a large office where three other Editors were making up magazines which were quietly fading into the Edwardian past, among them *The Royal* and once-popular *The Storyteller*.

On days when the sun reached the narrow side-streets between high newspaper buildings, I sauntered down past the race-touts at the corners, at lunch time, to the Embankment. There I watched the tugs with their trailing barges go by rapidly on the tide as if they were in a great hurry and the seagulls circling overhead. Often I thought of that fascinating line by Edmund Blunden; 'Near as Thames gulls and inaccessible as Dido's Phantom.'

When I came back from lunch, there was nothing to do. We talked, smoked, drowsed until afternoon tea.

After a month, I suggested that I should read in the British Museum for it was difficult to get sufficient books from the libraries. I made a few discoveries including *The Moment After*, a strange visional story, and *Eireadh of Canna*, a moving account of a woman on her way back to the Isles, both by Robert Buchanan, a Victorian writer who was never forgiven for his Puritanic essay *The Fleshly School of Poetry*.

V

One evening I received an unexpected invitation from Harold Monroe to the Poetry Book Shop in Museum Street. I had not seen him for some years since he moved with his gaily coloured wares from the drab Theobald's Road. There, appropriately enough, his shop was next to a goldbeater's den. Often as I stared at the latest chap-books in the window, I fancied that I could hear the small mallets softly beating out their spondees.

I wandered along Great Russell Street past unlit shop-windows, stopping to admire expensive art-books and oriental tomes on display. At last I came to the right number and turning left in the hallway, found myself in a large room where a crowd of men were watching in silence a Puppet Show. I waited for a few minutes, wondering why so many poets were interested in this rare amusement, before I ventured to ask a man near the door if I had come to the right place. He explained that this was the monthly meeting of the Marionette Society and that the Poetry Book Shop was upstairs on the first floor.

I left hastily for I was already late, and sitting half-way up on the stairs, met James Gould Fletcher and F. S. Flint, members of the Imagist Group which had so quickly dispersed itself. When I came into the room, it was already crowded and I stood at the door. My host shook hands, found me a chair, and brought me a glass of Rhenish wine. All were discussing poems and novels which had made them cry – from Lear's button, and Sterne's account of *Le Fevre to Uncle Tom's Cabin* and The Death of Little Nell. The mild wine seemed appropriate to the debate. Leaning against the mantelpiece, in the attitude of Mallarmé, on his famous Tuesday nights, was T. S. Eliot, tall, prim, bespectacled, studious in appearance. He said little of interest, but all turned to him respectfully whenever he made a remark. Glancing around with caution, I recognized most of the advanced critics. This was, in fact, the weekly meeting of the Criterion Circle which had so powerful an influence. It was easy to guess why I had been invited to its secret session. A month before, thanks to Humbert Wolfe, I had become a contributor to the Book Page of *The Observer*. It was edited by Violet Garvin and was one of the last defences of Tradition. I might be useful.

When all were leaving at about 11 o'clock, Harold Monroe asked me to stay on. He produced a bottle of Scotch for himself and a whole bottle of Rhenish wine for me. As he drank, he became more talkative and told me of his efforts throughout many years to spread an interest in poetry. During the 1914 War, he had been a 'fly boy' and was a tutor in County Tyrone. Perhaps he had been unhappy in a country house there, for he disliked Ireland. I thought him ungrateful, but could not help feeling sorry for him and flattered by his confidences as he complained of his thwarted ambition and his marriage.

When I was leaving in the small hours, he asked me to come again to the Criterion Circle, but I did not do so.

VI

Among the few poets I met at this time was that popular one, Alfred Noyes. I had reviewed a volume of his for *The Spectator* and he wrote inviting me to afternoon tea at his house in Regent's Park. As a modest indication that his own company might not be sufficient, he mentioned that Lady Asquith and a number of other titled ladies would be there. I arrived at the house in some trepidation and when a maid led me through a rather dingy hall, I almost fell over a large perambulator which was in the way. Unfortunately, Lady Asquith had been unable to come and the other titled ladies said little. Indeed, when the hospitable poet and his wife passed round the plates of cakes, those ladies showed astonishing avidity, and then with smiles and murmurs took their departure. I wondered whether they were all in reduced circumstances and were hurrying to other tea parties in order to empty more plates. When they were gone, the poet took me into his study and, seating himself behind a large mahogany writing-desk, read to me several long extracts from a new narrative poem in blank verse. He looked like an alert business man, his hair closely cropped, but he was an excellent reader, for he had recited his poems on many lecture tours throughout the United States. In his new poem, which dealt with the supposed conflict between Science and Religion, he described a shipwreck in mid-ocean and the first use of radio in sending out signals of distress. Although the theological implications were ingenious, I could not help thinking of Paley's Watch.

Alfred Noyes was a convert to Catholicism. The struggle had been a slow one, for he was very conscious of his stubborn ancestry. A John Noyes had been burned at the stake during the reign of

Bloody Mary for refusing to accept the doctrine of Transubstantiation. To equalize such matters, a later Noyes, who was a New England Divine, was a notorious witch-hunter and had caused several old women to be burned alive. Searching through the past, Alfred Noyes discovered that some of his forebears had not completely hated the old faith. Not without anxiety, he went to see Fr. Vincent McNabb and had several long talks with him: 'I was not sure how certain scientific doctrines which I believed to be true might be accounted heretical by Catholic theologians and when I discovered that the best Catholic Religious believed these doctrines themselves, with just that something more that allows the mind to make sense of the universe, I saw my way quite clearly'.

Delighted to find that the best Catholic theologians, unlike the worst, were men of liberal thought, open of mind, eager to discuss all subjects, the innocent Alfred Noyes decided to show his own broadmindedness by writing an unprejudiced study of Voltaire. This controversial book by a well-known convert was reviewed enthusiastically in the English Catholic press. When a second edition was about to be published, an anonymous letter-writer denounced the book to Rome. A good deal of trouble ensued and a letter from the Supreme Congregation of the Holy See led to the temporary suspension of the new edition. Alfred Noyes asserted very vigorously in a public statement that he was a twentieth-century Englishman – and there were almost bonfires in Belfast. It was clear that the poet who had written the epic of Elizabethan Protestantism in his earlier years was not to be deterred by the Holy Office. Through the intervention of Cardinal Pacelli, later Pope Pius XII, the matter was referred for settlement to Archbishop Hinsley. It transpired that there had been wrong translations in the correspondence over the matter and, in consequence, grievous misunderstanding. So all ended happily on earth – if not in Heaven.

VII

Harry Clarke, a namesake of mine, spent a winter in London and came round every week to visit me. He brought his own noggin of whisky for I could not afford him such hospitality after I had left *The Argosy*. He was a brilliant illustrator and stained-glass window artist in the Beardsley tradition. He had pictured with due horror and morbidity Poe's *Tales of Mystery and Imagination*. So I had suggested that he should illustrate merrily *The Intoxication of the Ulstermen*, based on an ancient mock-saga, *Mesca Uladh*, a long poem which I was writing. Unfortunately, the poem went wrong, for my technique had spread out too quickly.

The artist was tall, dark, handsome, consumptive. I have forgotten those evenings and can only remember the second last of them. When he arrived, he told me excitedly that he had discovered a tank in the back garden of his lodgings, full of tiny wriggling monsters, some of them scarcely visible. He was exalted for he saw in these microscopic shapes new forms for experiment in art. He would develop in ornamental designs these fantastic germ-shapes which had been almost hidden from the human eye for aeons.

Sometimes, I steal past the holy water font into Terenure Church to see the stained-glass window by Harry Clarke above the High Altar. Its hues are in delicate violet, green, purple: a glittering Celtic Twilight in which long-forgotten princesses and their lovers seem to sigh. It was commissioned by the late Father Healy, a man of culture, who met with much opposition in the parish but persisted.

On a morning when Father Healy was sitting in his parlour, one of his young curates rushed in, his face dark with morality.

'Father,' he exclaimed, 'you must stop these dances in the local hall. They are an occasion of shameless sin. Look what I have found.'

He flung on the table a handful of spent, shrivelled balloons.

VIII

After I had left *The Argosy*, it was depressing to return to the monthly round. Often I came away empty-handed from offices after the usual chat with a young Literary Assistant. I climbed the iron outer stairs of *The New Statesman* Office only too frequently to nothing. In the main office were bookshelves filled with rejects while the new books were kept in the sanctum. A languid young Assistant would invite me to look at what was on the shelves, knowing that I was well aware of the mean tricks. So I longed to escape from exile.

Though every office stair
I climbed there, left me poorer,
Night after night, my wants
Toil down each step in selfsame
Dream: night after night, enduring
Such failure, I cast away
My body, on fire to reach
Mail boat or train from Euston,
Catch up at last with smoke . . .

Twenty Five

THE SEVEN SISTERS' ROAD was dreary in the short winter light and only in reverie did I get as far as Angel Pavement. Often, I gazed at the 'Weekend Rings' in the small shops, made of brass and costing half-a-crown. They brought me amusing thoughts of Southend, the mud-flats, the mile-long Promenade, the stalls of scallops, the large hotels in which brass turned into gold at night. On the other side of the Thames estuary were more mud-flats, and inland, the marshes described by Charles Dickens in *Great Expectations.*

Little knowing that rents are higher in poor districts, my wife and I had taken a flat in a side-street off the Seven Sisters' Road, not far from the gloomy Brides-in-the-Bath house.

The rooms were quiet and I did not suspect for some weeks that a couple of prostitutes were living upstairs. At night, we could hear feet lumbering up the stairs into silence. Every Saturday morning, a sports car waited outside and one of the girls in gay dress drove off with a young man for the weekend. Regularly on every Friday, the landlady arrived for her rent.

Early in the spring, we decided to live in the country, but there was a difficulty. I had signed a contract to stay a year. Suddenly I saw the way out of town, and one morning, paid a surprise visit to the fine villa at Primrose Hill. The landlady brought me into her drawing-room with a smile. When I told her why I had come, her face became grim. Getting up, with hat and stick, I said in a stern Victorian tone: 'Well then, I'm going straight down to the L.C.C. to report that you're keeping a house of ill-fame'.

She was startled for a moment, but quickly picked up her wits. She assured me that she was a widow, innocent of the way of the world, having lived all her life in Somerset. She had only been ten years in London. She continued to plead and protest. Nevertheless, nen I left, a letter terminating the contract was in my breast pocket.

Bricketwood, which was a few miles from the city of St. Albans, consisted of a grocer's shop and a small Methodist chapel with a roof of galvanized iron, painted red. A leafy corner protected by several great demesnes. In the nearby woods, divided by rides, were bungalows and shacks. Early in the morning the owners travelled on the side-branch to Watford and London. They were kindly, quiet people; all worked in their gardens on Sunday except the few Methodists.

Opposite the bungalow which we rented in Lye Lane, an ancient Roman water-course still glistened across the fields in the early Spring, so alluringly that I could not find a metaphor for it. In wet weather our garden was flooded and we had to venture to the halldoor on planks laid across large stones. The dykes at each side of Lye Lane brimmed with water in which the last yeoman of Hertfordshire might have been drowned a century ago. Ornamental shrubs had been planted in our garden to bloom in turn throughout most of the year, such as winter jasmine, guelder rose, barbary, flowering currant, lilac, laburnum, forsythia.

Above the long path at the back of the bungalow was an eleven-acre field which I could use. It had lofty hedges and behind the southern one was a Nudist Colony. Often I thought of the Adamite sects who tried to recover the primal innocence. Prodicus founded a colony in the second century. The Brethren of the Free Spirit, in the fourteenth century, cast off their clouts and rejected wedlock. A hundred years later, more Adamites sprang up in Bohemia. All were soon massacred.

The summer was unusually hot. The cos lettuces grew longer, seeded in a rush. The plum tree, trestled along the sunniest wall of the bungalow, was heavy with fruit already purpling. I longed to plunge into the swimming pool at the Colony for the Superintendent had invited me to use it any time I wished. Unfortunately, there was a strict rule that no bathing costume should be worn. I recalled at once the words of St. Augustine regarding an ideal state, had there been no Fall: 'Man therefore would have sown his seed, and woman received it, as need required without all lust and as their wills desired: for, as we now are, our articulated members do not only obey our will, our hands or feet or so, but even those also that we move, only by small sinews or tendons, we contract and turn them

194

as we list. Even so might man have had obedience of his lower p
which his own disobedience debarred. For God could have eas
made him with all his members subject to his will, even that whic
is now not moved only by lust'.

A friend who sunbathed at the Colony explained to me how he acquired gradually, after some embarrassing experiences, the method of self-control. Pleasantly, too, he described some of the minor disadvantages of nudity. At his first naked tea-party, he felt uncomfortable owing to the cake crumbs. Glancing down, the girl beside him smiled and handed him a comb from her toilet bag.

I admired the self-control of the nudists in their enclosure and envied that higher state of being known to them. So I endeavoured to express all this indirectly in a novel of the Celtic-Romanesque era, in a vision of the glorified body after the Resurrection.

Often on a summer's evening, I watched from our bay-window the Adamites coming to the Colony on motor-cycle combinations. Most of them were solemn, plain-faced. Sometimes a young couple hesitated at the discreet gate and I guessed that they were in search of the Midnight Sun.

Although London was only twenty miles away, it took more than an hour to reach it from the small station at Bricketwood. Among the few who came down to see us were Madame Cogley, one of the founders of the Dublin Gate Theatre, R. N. D. Wilson, Harry Kernoff, the painter. R. N. D. Wilson had become a convert when Yeats called for a Neo-Catholic School after Iseult Gonne had read some of the poetry of Claudel, Péguy and Jammes to him. Francis Stuart, I think, and some others were also re-baptized. I admired that formal lyric, *St. Apollinare in Classe* by R. N. D. Wilson, in which he described the westward flight of religion:

> Thought swarmed here once: the stark
> - Thebaid brake its comb,
> And poured out of the dark
> Wild honey to Rome, –
>
> Then, as of old,
> The skies of Patmus dipt;
> Very gold of very gold
> Glowed in the crypt,

And flawless, lit with green
Cool light as from a wave,
The sea-veined cipolline
Pillared the nave.

What sweetness ventured thus
To tempt Theology
To build her such a house,
Or set the daring bee

So wide to rove, that men
Have never wholly lost
The gold that clustered then
About the Host?

Somewhere among my papers is a strange poem by R. N. D. Wilson, which was not published at the time. It moved me because of its verbal music and compassion. It told of a youth who escaped from the burning city of Sodom, crossed the plain and reached the mountains. Half-naked, bruised by boulders, cut by flints, he was found by a shepherd who carried him tenderly with kisses to his hut and succoured him.

Food in the country was little better than in the great City. Butter, eggs, ham, bacon, tea, were of inferior quality. Beef, mutton, were chilled or frozen. We were forced to deal in the most expensive shop in the market square of St. Albans, where old ladies, helped in by chauffeurs from their cars, gave large weekly orders. One shop, founded more than a century ago, maintained the tradition of good fare; we bought there wonderful pork pies and veal-and-ham pies. The journey to St. Albans was often hazardous for the regular bus and the 'pirate' one raced in competition, so that I had to stagger by the seats upstairs to bang the bell and bring our bus to a stop.

The last agricultural labourer in Bricketwood came weekly to start the small petrol engine which pumped water into the roof-tank. He was a lithe, active man in his thirties, who was employed by the owner of a large residence. He earned a few pounds a week and when he asked for a slight increase, he met with a stern refusal. He decided to give up the job, but his employer notified wealthy friends in the neighbourhood and so he could not find other work. I urged him to go farther afield but in vain. Despite his war service, he was still a serf.

Once a month an elderly gardener came to tidy the flowerbeds. He was as careful in his enunciation as in his raking and scuffling.

'Would you like me to clip the hedges or the edges?' he asked me one afternoon.

Shortly after our arrival, there was political excitement in the nearby woods. A Socialist, who had settled in them, was elected to the City Council of St. Albans which was notorious for its jobbery and corruption. In his first speech in the Council Chamber, he denounced the wickedness of his fellow-members who were all Tories. To his amazement, they agreed with all his plans for immediate reform. Some weeks later his daughter became private secretary to the owner of a big estate. The new member never recovered. Sometimes, I saw him straying by himself along the edge of the local wilderness of scrub-oak, into which none had penetrated for centuries.

II

At Townsend, in a row of neat artisan dwellings on a height outside St. Albans, Herbert Palmer lived. Across the valley on the slope was the mansion which Dickens had used as the setting for *Bleak House*. A keen observer could have discovered the poet's humble abode for it was the only one which had no crazy pavement in front. When the council workmen arrived with mortar and new tiles, the poet threw their buckets, trowels, picks, over the little railings. They fled from the wrath of this Minor Prophet and avoided his gate after that.

Herbert Palmer was thin, puny-faced, steel-bespectacled and most excitable. When a barber in St. Albans refused very rightly to shave him because of a rash, he came back at midnight with a brick and hurled it through the shop window. Several Aldermen had to intervene privately to keep the poet out of court. I did not meet him too often, because I never knew what catastrophe would occur. When I came to his house for the first time, he brought me up to his den after our Nonconformist High Tea. He fumbled with the Aladdin lamp, carbonized it, and in a moment, dense black fumes surrounded us, hiding the bookshelves and the litter of manuscripts.

His gentle, patient wife hurried upstairs and rescued us from the murk. Sometimes, we drank at the Cock Tavern, the smallest in England: it had been used as a fishing retreat in the Middle Ages by the monks from the massive monastery on the hill above. Colne Spring, the local beer, was so strong that after three bottles of it, we found or lost ourselves in Merrie England.

Once when Seumas O'Sullivan was on a visit to London, he invited both of us to lunch at a Soho restaurant. When the poet arrived, he had a woebegone expression on his face.

'I set on moy teeth in the troin and broke 'em,' he exclaimed in his Cockney accent.

While he was hanging up his overcoat, I worked out quickly a menu of pap: clear soup, ravioli, zabaglione, a flask of Chianti. The toothless poet ate, talked rapidly, without realizing that all had been made easy for him.

III

When my wife and I returned to Dublin with our two small children, Herbert Palmer came to stay with us for a fortnight at Templeogue. He was an expert fisherman and had written a delightful book on angling. So, on his first evening, he hurried down to the river at the end of the garden, but caught only a few fingerlings. He spent almost every day fishing along the sandy reaches of the King's River near Blessington. I knew well those tiny creeks before the new reservoir was made and once at night, as a sleepy child, I had seen Will o'the Wisp leaping across the boglands – the last Tudor trying to escape to the Pale.

We were never certain when the poet would return with his fishing tackle and empty basket. Once, as I waited at Templeogue Bridge, I saw him alone in the 65 bus, a heavenly expression on his face, being carried towards the City. On the first Sunday afternoon, we brought him to a friend's house, a few fields away. Off the drawing-room was a conservatory with a heavily laden vine. The poet stopped in astonishment.

'Gripes in the 'ouse!' he exclaimed.

That memorable saying remained with us long after he was gone. Herbert Palmer was an unusual poet. His work was a complete

expression of his disassociating, symbolic individuality. The jingle
of Kipling, snatches of psalmody, glees, jubilant satiric strains were
all carried along in his lines. *Summit aud Chasm*, the title of one of
his collections was typical. If he were not struggling towards the
heights, he was tumbling into some awful chasm of poetic diction.

He had a small civil list pension which made him unhappy, for
he had to pay income tax on it. During the Second World War, he
moulded a leaden sonnet about Winston Churchill. Despite his vast
responsibilities, the Statesman picked up the public pen and at a
stroke increased the pension to the fine sum of three hundred pounds
a year.

Herbert Palmer was obsessed by his hatred of Modernism and
suspected that I was not free from its dire influence – long before I
was aware of this myself. It took me many years before I was able
to write about the present age, and when I did so, I found that other
poets had retired to the campus and quadrangle, having rejected the
belief that writers should be concerned with social reform.

Herbert Palmer was unceremonious with his Muse:

> Lean over me now, Fafeenee
> For the Devil is standing by,
> And the pantry door is open,
> And it's filled with the blue fly.
> Let the meat foul the blade and the white salt turn grey,
> We two shall be one forever when the world has passed
> away.

He tired of unreal idealists who 'hoist Heaven's dejected Dove'.

> Now for new words strange reflex to your praise
> Down with the strumpet, I am tired of Love.

Always there was the visional flash:

> Songs Eglantine, the hyacinth cupola
> Or the juniper, Elijah's cloaking Tower.

Twenty Six

I

ONE SATURDAY MORNING during the 'Thirties, I had an urgent telephone call from *The Times Literary Supplement* to which I was a regular contributor. W. B. Yeats was dangerously ill on the Riviera. Could I write a leader on his work of about three thousand words? It was a difficult task, but I had to set my mind to it. On Sunday night, I had finished dictating the article and my wife typed it. On Monday morning, I was on my way to London with the three-and-a-half columns in my pocket. Happily the poet recovered and so the obituary was not used until some years had gone by.

Sometime after that, I was asked by a publishing firm to write a biographical study of Yeats. Despite the great reputation of the poet as a Nobel Prize-winner, only three studies of his work had appeared: the first, a short one, by an American critic, the other two by Irishmen, J. M. Hone, and the novelist, Forrest Reid. The alert young director who interviewed me lit a cigarette and asked me whether the love affair between Maud Gonne and Yeats had been platonic or not, as this would give interest to the book and help to sell it.

'I'll find out,' I said.

'How?'

'I'll ask Yeats.'

The director looked at me with such surprise that I realized at once the rashness of my promise.

When I got back to Bricketwood, I took down from a shelf *The Wind among the Reeds* and read it carefully in order to see if I could find out the truth from the poems themselves. These lyrics have the languorous, sensuous quality which the poets of the 'Nineties borrowed from the Pre-Raphaelites. Certainly in some of them there were indications that the poet's relations with Maud Gonne had been immoral!

> Passion-dimmed eyes and long heavy hair
> That was shaken out over my breast.

And again:

> White woman that passion has worn
> As the tide wears the dove-grey sands.

Had there not been unkind gossip about her supposed affairs with European diplomats?

In one of the poems, 'The Lover Speaks to the Hearers of his Songs in Coming Days', I seemed among those hearers as I read the line:

> Bend down and pray for all that sin I wove in song.

I sat for a long time wondering over the character of Yeats and recalling the various occasions on which I had met him.

At Coole, where he was staying after his marriage, he had spoken to me at length of Donne, Vaughan, and then of Landor, his voice rising and falling in a chant as he urged me to study their works and follow their austere example. As I was a lecturer in English Literature at the time in University College, Dublin, and still immersed in Gaelic mythology and poetry, his severe address chilled me. To vary a well-known remark, I felt that I had met Yeats too late and Joyce too soon.

When Yeats returned to Dublin, I saw him every Thursday evening during the following winter at the house of Joseph O'Neill, Secretary to the Department of Education and a very original novelist. Yeats was then writing *A Vision*. Women crowded around him in that drawing-room, listening eagerly as he discussed the book with them. Across the room I could hear his monotonous tones: 'One may regard the subjective phases as forming a separate wheel. Its phase 8 between phases 11 and 12 . . . of the larger wheel, its phase 22 between phases 19 and 20. . . .' I turned to talk to others, but I could still hear that chanting voice: 'The true *Creative Mind* of phase 27 I describe as super sensual receptivity and it is derived from phase 3 as that phase is modified by its *Body of Fate*'. I disliked astrology, horoscope casting and other follies of the past and so during that winter I carefully avoided the poet on these occasions. One night, however, I found myself walking home after midnight with him and Iseult, the beautiful daughter of Maud Gonne. They talked happily together and I felt an intruder as I kept up with their rapid pace for both were long-legged. As we were passing Harcourt Street Railway Station, I glanced at them furtively and they seemed so much alike that I could not help wondering whether the rumours that they were father and daughter were correct. Later I learned that this literary legend of Dublin was completely false.

I wrote to Yeats asking whether he would approve of my wish to write a biographical study of him and would be kind enough to see me some time at his convenience, when I was over in Dublin. While I waited for a reply from him, I started to collect material for the work and went to the Reading Room of the British Museum three or four times a week. I piled the pretty books of the 'Nineties on the desk beside me, and, as I read through them, I was surprised to find how alike the poets of that time were in tone and cadence.

Ernest Dowson used the difficult Alexandrine measure with extraordinary skill and Yeats was surely influenced by him. An *Epigram* of his seems to have anticipated the austerity of the Irish poet in his middle period:

> Because I am idolatrous and have besought,
> With grievous supplication and consuming prayer,
> The admirable image that my dreams have wrought
> Out of her swan's neck and her dark, abundant hair:
> The jealous gods, who brook no worship save their own,
> Turned my live idol marble and her heart to stone.

I became interested in theosophy, dipped into Synnott's *Buddhism*, several books by Madame Blavatsky, explored Rosicrucianism and the nineteenth-century outbreak of Satanism in France. I read books by Maeterlinck, Loti, and the early novels of Huysmans, Pierre MacOrlan and others.

Six weeks had gone by and still I had not received a reply from Yeats, but I did not worry for I knew that he was not a quick correspondent. When I had written my first verse play, then called *Black Fast*, I sent it to the Abbey Theatre, waited patiently for six months and then wrote to enquire about it. The comedy came back to me with a note from Lennox Robinson, who was then Manager of the Theatre, and a brief comment on it by Yeats. The comment was so badly typed that I suspect one or the other of them had poked it out on a machine which needed urgent repairs. The comment, which depressed me very much, was as follows: 'I return Austin Clarke's play. It has imagination, a sense of turbulent grotesque life, but it would not play. An audience would not understand the central idea and so it would lack coherence. I think that Austin Clarke has had two rival art forms competing with one another: (1) the verse drama (2) the picturesque prose drama. I think that the play left to itself would have changed from (1) to (2). Open the play by chance at page 4, surely the natural rhythm here is prose rhythm and the line endings and the blank verse break up this rhythm without imposing their own. The very first words on the page prove my point:

> 'He was roaring in (line ends)
> The Kitchen'

If he was to recreate in prose and disengage the central idea, he might make an interesting play. I suppose the central idea is hunger as contrasted with the poet's dream or some dream, but I am not sure. A work of art can have only one subject and there must be perfect clarity – at least to the subconscious mind – in the representation of the idea.

You can send any of this you like to Clarke.'

I hasten to add that I had deliberately used a very free rhythm in parts of the play – which was produced later with reasonable success at the Cambridge Festival Theatre.

No reply to a second note had come and three months had almost elapsed. In despair, I called to see Robert Lynd, Literary Editor of the *News Chronicle*.

'If it was a duchess who had written to him, a reply would have come to her at once,' sneered Lynd. The sudden bitterness of so amiable an essayist surprised me for I had forgotten at the moment how many writers were irritated by the aloofness and aristocratic manner of Yeats. I decided to write once more to Dublin for I had come to a decision about the biography. The return railway fare, third class, from Bricketwood to Euston was 2*s*. 6*d*. and my lunch at one of the small restaurants owned by polite elderly ladies or widows in the vicinity of Great Portland Street was usually 1*s*. 11*d*. At this rate of expenditure, the fifty pounds advance on royalties promised to me by the publisher would not last long. Elbows on desk, I had hurried through a hundred books about the period and was still searching confusedly for an explanation of the charm of the 'Nineties. How could so many literary movements in Europe have all appeared during the ten years of the *fin de siècle*? One happy morning, I received a note from the great man to tell me that he would be in London during the following week and would meet me in the Savile Club at four o'clock on the Tuesday afternoon of that week.

II

In the sedate, gloomy lounge of the Savile Club, W. B. Yeats was seated alone at a small tea-table, already waiting for me. He got up at once, shook hands with me, and spoke at once.

'I am over in London for a few days to arrange about the publication of my new book, *A Vision*, which has taken me many years to write. I have no doubt that the critics and philosophers will not agree with what I have said in it, but I am sure that I am right in my theory of the universe.'

He remained standing for a few moments, his head bowed in humility, looking so absurd that I could not help smiling secretly to myself. Somehow I could not believe in this new pose but I have no doubt that he felt a little anxious about the reception which the book would get because of its strange admixture of philosophy, astrology and abracadabra. He could not have guessed that in later years his theories would be analysed respectfully by professors and students with scant knowledge of the follies of the past. When he sat down, a waiter appeared immediately and the poet ordered tea. Then, much to my surprise, in a stern reproachful tone, he said: 'This is not an interview and on no account must anything I say be given to the press.' He added, however, in a milder tone and with a smile, 'When I was a younger writer, I frequently attacked the journalists, but since then I have learnt to tolerate them'.

As I was only a book reviewer and much too impracticable to be

204

a Fleet Street journalist, his suspicions made me uneasy – all the more so as I had before me the difficult problem of asking him about his relations with Maud Gonne.

We had scarcely begun to talk when, much to my alarm, I saw Sir John Squire, poet, critic, former editor of the *London Mercury* and literary dictator, coming into the lounge. He hurried over to Yeats and began talking to him. After a minute or so he turned to me and asked agreeably, 'How is your Celtic Empire getting on, Clarke?' For a moment I was puzzled and then I remembered the evening I had spent with him some years previously at his house in Chiswick. As we sat in his small, book-lined study upstairs drinking beer, he spoke unsympathetically of the Irish struggle for freedom. Provoked by his attitude and slightly intoxicated by the mild-and-bitter, to which I was not accustomed, I described rapidly a great Celtic Empire spreading to England, the Colonies and the United States of America. I had forgotten long since my horrible vision of a corrupting, powerful Tammany Hall – our contribution to modern civilization. Fortunately, Yeats remained aloof, and, seeing that he was not wanted, Sir John left us and strolled into the bar room.

We returned to our conversation and I mentioned Forrest Reid's book.

'I have forgotten it,' intoned Yeats, gently waving away that invisible volume with his right hand, on which gleamed a large signet ring of silver made for him by Edmund Dulac. No doubt my own study would be forgotten as quickly, I thought, and my depression increased. He became cheerful again and said to me as if by rote, 'There are portraits of me in the National Gallery in Merrion Square, and also in the Dublin Municipal Art Gallery. There are others in the galleries of Liverpool, Birmingham, Bristol, Leicester and Edinburgh'.

This was not very helpful but he mentioned soon afterwards that few critics had written about his plays and it was clear that he wished me to deal specially with them. As I had always admired his plays very much, I agreed with him about the critics. I would have liked to have told him of those early years when I had seen many of them at the Abbey Theatre, but I hesitated and the opportunity passed. There was a lull in our conversation and I knew the dire moment had come when I must ask about Maud Gonne. Carefully wrapping up my question in as many vague words as was possible, I said: 'Mr. Yeats, I would like to discuss with you *The Wind among the Reeds*, a book which I have always liked immensely. It would help me very much in writing my study to have a general idea of your inclinations in those love-poems. Would it be too much to ask if there is any basis in actual fact for them?'

Yeats caught my implication at once. His manner changed and, looking down at me like an eminent Victorian, he exclaimed: 'Sir, are you trying to pry into my private life?' Then, seeing my startled expression, he must have felt that he had gone too far, for in a trice, he had become confidential and, smiling pleasantly, continued with a vague wave of the hand. 'Of course, if you wish to suggest something in your biography, you may do so, provided that you do not write anything that would give offence to any persons living'.

As a Victorian, he wanted to have it both ways. Unfortunately, during his interview, I was sitting close to Yeats on the inner side of the small table and occasionally, as I turned to him, I could see behind the thick lens of his glasses a brown eye straining at its tiny muscles as if trying to peep into my very thoughts. It was the cute eye of a Sligo man and yet it seemed, somehow, to have an existence of its own. Every time I saw that small watcher, I turned away in embarrassment. About five o'clock he appeared fatigued and said the time had come for him to lie down and rest before dinner. He stood gazing into space as I put on my overcoat, took my hat and stick, and then said farewell to me at the entrance of the lounge.

I never wrote the book.

II

When I came back to live in Templeogue, I thought often of 'The Wild Old Man' a little more than a mile away in his house at Rathfarnham, knocking impatiently on his bedroom wall at seven o'clock in the morning for his cup of tea: I seemed to see him, too, carefully wrapped, being wheeled in his bath-chair along the shady road to Billy's Bridge. Bravely, he declaimed against 'bodily decrepitude' and sang his songs of the ilium.

Nevertheless, Yeats was still interested in the unseen, drawn by hands held in the dark and voice-changing. How many Sludges had

satisfied their curiosity, hopped, one after the other, over the ridge. But the hare remained – so long indeed, that I thought he would never go. So as the sun was moving westward, I ended the musical test abruptly.'

'You speak of the harmonica, but there is a line in a poem of yours called *The Fair at Windgap*, which has puzzled me very much, "the ha'penny harp that is played on a finger".'

'I meant the Jew's harp.

Moore looked blank.

'It is rather hard to describe,' I went on. 'It is a small metal instrument, held between the teeth and strummed by one finger.'

'I'm sure,' said Longworth, 'that Clarke believes it is an ancient oriental instrument, sadly reduced in price and size. Actually the name is only a corruption of the prosaic phrase, "jaw's harp".'

The sunlight had left the sill when Mabel, the housekeeper, came to announce dinner. As we went down the narrow staircase, past walls lined with small engravings and etchings, I was still wondering whether the motor cyclist had really exploded down Ebury Street that evening. George Moore had depicted the plight of the young sparrow so tenderly, so thoughtfully, that the little bird might have been a remote descendant of Philip, the pet sparrow, whom Skelton's nun fed from her own lips. Had he graciously invented the little episode in order to put me at my ease? Was it, perhaps, a passage from his new romance *Aphrodite in Aulis*, the sparrow being affrighted by the fall of some block of marble?

When we came back to the drawing-room after dinner, the blinds were drawn and, in a soft shaded light, we forgot the rumbling sounds of London. Much to my surprise and pleasure, George Moore suddenly took a book of mine from a small table.

'I like that poem in which you re-tell the old Gaelic legend of Craftiné. A musician's wife fled with her lover, and both were pursued by the mysterious sound of music and could never find peace. I have marked the page and I'll read two stanzas:

> Evening was paler
> Than leaves of the foxglove,
> When from sedges of forest,
> It happened those lovers,
> Who had come to the water

209

Where moonlight was mooring,
Unfastened the saddle
And thought to have rest.

Where the otter
Sank into jewels,
By the ferries of forest
They heard strange music
Cross: one of them wept
For, at Tara, she knew
Her husband was playing on
The hole-headed flute.

His voice had become severe.

'What disturbs me is the first line of that second stanza. There is one syllable missing in it.'

'That was deliberate. It was an attempt to suggest the sudden drop as the otter dives under water, leaving bubbles and bright circles above him.'

'No, no,' exclaimed Moore. 'The lines in every stanza should match.'

I argued the point, but slowly realised that the master of the most subtle rhythm in modern prose would permit no liberty to verse.

'There is a syllable missing,' he grumbled half to himself.

With a lawyer's tact, Longworth intervened. 'Clarke was telling me the other day of a very interesting medieval Irish poem about harps.'

'Can you remember any of it? Will you bring me a translation of it the next time you come?' Moore's voice was full of curiosity and excitement. 'I was in great difficulties about a harper when I was writing *Ulick and Soracha*. And now I must re-write the story. I see from your own book that you have written a poem about *The Frenzy of Sweeny*. That tale inspired half my own book, and none of the critics noticed the fact. *The Frenzy of Sweeny* is one of the great stories of the world, and yet how many know of its existence? There is no more local colour in it than in Theocritus – yet was Nature ever so near, so wild and so tender? A King of Ireland cursed by a saint because he refused to give him land to build another church. He wanders witlessly through the woods, living on cress, herbs,

210

berries and spring water. He hears the stag, 'the little bleating one, the melodious little clamourer'. He shelters by the sharp holly, 'a door against the wind'. He dreads the ash tree because it is used for making 'weapons of war'.

'And when his senses are returning to him,' I exclaimed, 'he is looked after by the Hag of the Mill.'

'The crazy conversation of the old crone brings back his madness. The tattered couple rush out and race together, playing hopscotch over the hills. And centuries before Shakespeare confronted Lear and Gloucester, that unknown storyteller brought the madman of Ireland across the sea to meet the madman of Britain, and the two old men wandered together in torment through those other woods.'

'Only recently,' Moore went on, 'I discovered for myself one of the great neglected themes of our history – Bruce's dream of a Celtic hegemony. But I am too old to write that story of an enterprise which almost succeeded. You must write a play about it, and when you come again, we will talk of nothing but the Ireland of the Bruces.'

The hour grew late as we moved through stories forgotten even in our own country. Longworth, ever the watchful lawyer, glanced at me significantly. It was time to leave. The aged writer had grown suddenly tired, and the light was gone from his face. But the lingering gentleness of his expression made me forget my previous ridiculous impressions of him that evening.

George Moore came down with us and, drawing me aside, pointed to a door off the hall. 'You may want a pumpship.'

I was so surprised by his use of a coarse nautical metaphor, so agitated, that I hurt two of my fingers between the narrow door and jamb.

As Colonel Longworth and I walked towards the bus row at Victoria Station, one of my fingers was still aching.

So ended my first Conversation at Ebury Street.

Index

213

215